OXFORD ENGLISH MONOGRAPHS

General Editors

NORMAN DAVIS   HELEN GARDNER

ALICE WALKER

OXFORD ENGLISH MONOGRAPHS

A GLASTONBURY MISCELLANY
OF THE
FIFTEENTH CENTURY

A DESCRIPTIVE INDEX OF

Trinity College, Cambridge, MS. O.9.38

BY

A. G. RIGG

OXFORD UNIVERSITY PRESS

1968

Oxford University Press, Ely House, London W. 1

GLASGOW NEW YORK TORONTO MELBOURNE WELLINGTON
CAPE TOWN SALISBURY ,BADAN NAIROBI LUSAKA ADDIS ABABA
BOMBAY CALCUTTA MADRAS KARACHI LAHORE DACCA
KUALA LUMPUR SINGAPORE HONG KONG TOKYO

PRINTED IN GREAT BRITAIN

PREFACE

IN the introduction to the recent *Supplement* to the *Index of Middle English Verse* the Editors remarked on a current trend in medieval literary studies towards 'complete editions of Middle English manuscripts... focusing attention on the problems of the whole manuscript—in other words, a trend from the poem in isolation to the poems in society'. The present work may be seen as part of such a trend. The great variety among the entries in Trinity College, Cambridge, MS. O.9.38 makes it an invaluable index to the taste of at least one fifteenth-century reader, its anonymous Glastonbury compiler. My doctoral thesis, of which the present volume is a condensation, was a full edition of most of the contents of the manuscript. The publication of the entire contents, however, would have been not only impractical but also unnecessary: individual entries may be of interest to scholars in separate fields (and several of the previously unknown ones have been, or are being, printed in various journals), but for anyone primarily concerned with some specific area of medieval studies the length of a full edition would have been an obstacle to the over-all appreciation of the nature of the collection. On the other hand, a bare contents list would be inadequate to reveal the nature of many of the items, or to inform the reader of the scribe's methods of working.

As a compromise, therefore, I conceived the idea of the present 'Descriptive Index'. The Introduction describes the appearance of the manuscript, its history, language, literary interest, etc.; this is followed by the 'Index' proper, which consists of a brief account of each entry and sufficient biblio-graphical information to make further investigation possible. The manuscript can, however, be localized firmly, and in order to emphasize the fact that it originated at a specific time in a specific place, I include in Appendix I full editions of those entries which associate the collection with Glastonbury.

A somewhat unusual procedure has been followed with the bibliography: so many references were part of the general equipment of the descriptions that it seemed otiose to include both a list of abbreviations and a separate bibliography: the Bibliographical Index has therefore been made to serve both purposes, without, I hope, too great an inconvenience to the reader.

I am grateful to the Master and Fellows of Trinity College, Cambridge, for permission to edit their manuscript, and particularly to the librarians of the College for their help and courtesy. In preparing for edition a collection of items of such varied kinds, I have all too frequently been obliged to call on the aid of many scholars of medieval literature, history, and music, to all of whom I owe my most sincere thanks: Professors Robert W. Ackerman and Thurston Dart, Dr. Martin Evans, Mr. Richard Hamer, Mrs. Rachel Hands, Dr. Frank Harrison, Dr. Roger Highfield, Dr. W. A. Pantin, and Dr. R. H. Robbins (who made available to me much of the material for the *Supplement* to the *Index* before its publication). My botanical knowledge was supplied almost entirely by Mr. R. M. Sidaway. I am glad to have had the opportunity of discussing the manuscript with the late Dr. F. J. E. Raby. Library staffs of England, Scotland, and America—particularly that of the Bodleian—have given me great assistance and service. My wife has not only given me constant encouragement, but helped me considerably in the preparation of the original thesis.

To those who know him and have benefited from his knowledge and his selfless and good-humoured attention, it is sufficient to say that Professor Norman Davis has superintended my work, both as the supervisor of my thesis and as the Editor of this series. His tireless scrutiny has saved me from many errors, omissions, and infelicities: no acknowledgement could adequately express the enormous debt that I owe him.

A.G.R.

California
March 1968

CONTENTS

INTRODUCTION

DESCRIPTION OF THE MANUSCRIPT

TRINITY COLLEGE, Cambridge, MS. O.9.38[1] belongs to the collection (shelf-mark O) donated to the library in 1738 by Roger Gale. It is a paper volume, measuring $11\frac{3}{4} \times 4\frac{1}{4}$ in.: this size of book was suitable for carrying in a holster[2] and was often used for keeping accounts (cf. the first entry in the MS.). In its present binding it consists of the following leaves: i–iii, 1–89, iv–vi. The fly-leaves (unmarked) and binding are of the seventeenth or eighteenth century; the binding is of a purple-grey cardboard with a white, imitation-vellum spine (a common binding among MSS. of the Gale collection), and the spine is now falling apart. The front half of the original soft vellum folder is extant, and precedes f. 1: written on the inside of it is an incomplete list of contents, probably by Gale (see below pp. 6–7). The collation of the leaves appears[3] to be: 1[8], 2–6[6], 7[8] (leaves have been cut out in the third gathering after f. 36, in the sixth after f. 74, and in the last after f. 87); about half an inch has been cut from the bottom of the folder and f. 1, just over an inch from the top of f. 69, and f. 88 has been cut right down to

---

[1] The contents of the MS. were edited in full by me as a thesis for the degree of D.Phil. (Oxford, 1966) entitled 'An Edition of a Fifteenth Century Commonplace Book (Trinity College, Cambridge, MS. O.9.38)', vol. i, 'Introduction, Text', vol. ii, 'Notes, Appendix, Glossaries'. Copies of the thesis are now deposited in the Bodleian Library, Oxford, and Trinity College, Cambridge. A brief description of the MS. and a list of its contents are given by James, *Catalogue*, iii. 495–502. The MS. (main hand) is referred to throughout as **T**.

[2] F. Wormald and C. E. Wright, *The English Library before 1700* (1958), pp. 55, 64, list other examples of 'literary' holster-books, one of which is Balliol MS. 354: see below, pp. 23, 26.

[3] I have been unable to verify the collation properly, for fear of damaging the binding and the paper any further. The gatherings, which have no catch-words, were probably unbound until modern times: gatherings 1, 2, 3, 4, and 6 all begin with a new entry (ff. 1, 17, 29, 40, 64). Gathering 5, however, begins (on f. 52[a]) in the middle of No. xxviii, which occupies ff. 49[b]–54[a]. It is impossible to be certain where the last gathering begins.

a small square only three inches high at the bottom of the page.[1] The missing leaves after ff. 36 and 74 and the inch missing from the top of f. 69 were all absent when the first scribe wrote in the MS.

The MS. is in extremely poor condition, as it was in 1729 when Hearne described it as 'very rotten' (cf. also below, p. 8). The most serious damage is at the end: the outer edge of the last fifteen folios is badly frayed, and on about f. 71 the top outer corner has begun to fray, so that by the end of the MS. the whole of the top corner is missing; there is a tear about $1\frac{1}{2}$ in. long from the middle of the outer edge on ff. 75 to the end, which by f. 78 has widened into a wedge-shaped gap and by the end of the MS. has become a large triangle. Only a fragment of the last leaf, f. 89, remains: the bottom half has disappeared entirely, and fraying has reduced the remainder to a crescent-shaped piece about 6 in. long. The deterioration cannot have begun until after 1561, the date of Appendix II No. *14 by hand **A**, whose writing must originally have covered all the back page, but had begun when Twyne examined the MS. (see below, p. 7).

The rapid deterioration in less than 180 years suggests that some time between 1561 and 1634 the MS. was allowed to get very wet: a large damp blot, about $5\frac{1}{2} \times 3\frac{1}{2}$ in. on f. 1, affects the first eight leaves and makes the verso sides particularly illegible; from f. 49 onwards there is a damp stain across the top of the page, about $\frac{3}{4}$ in. wide; the outer edge of the leaves from f. 54 is marked by damp, which has no doubt contributed to the serious fraying. Damp has often affected the colour of the ink of hands **T**, **X**, and **A**. The paper is still fraying badly, which has made the handling of the MS. very difficult, particularly at the points where it is most illegible.

The modern pencil foliation continues from 1 to 89: ff. 62–8 were incorrectly numbered 63–9, but corrected; James, however,

---

[1] The pencilled foliation, followed by James, numbers ff. 88 and 89 respectively 89 and 88, but close examination shows that the badly damaged f. 89 (by my renumbering) is in fact the last leaf of the MS.

has been misled by the error: subtract 1 from all his references from f. 63ᵃ to the end.

Three watermarks are found on the paper: a single tower, with windows and door, set in a hexagonal oblong shield c. $1\frac{1}{2} \times 1$ in. (ff. 6, 9, 16, 19, 24, 27); a sickle c. $2\frac{1}{2}$ in. long (ff. 34, 35, 38, 42, 44, 50, 53, 54, 56, 65, 66, 70); a hand, gauntleted, fingers together, thumb outspread, also $2\frac{1}{2}$ in. long (ff. 83, 85, 89). None of the armorial towers in Briquet,[1] Nos. 2267 ff., resembles this one; none, for instance, has a window. The sickle, however, is exactly like Briquet No. 6150 (Luxemburg 1478 and Utrecht 1480: Briquet ii, 356) and similar to Mošin and Traljić[2] Nos. 3797 (1380–4) and 3799 (1387); from Briquet's remarks it seems likely that, although the sickle mark originated in Italy, it was also being used independently in the Low Countries. The gloved hand is very close to Briquet No. 11080 (Pignerol 1389), which had a wide provenance, including the Netherlands, from 1389 till the middle of the fifteenth century (Briquet iii, 562–4); it is also similar to Mošin and Traljić Nos. 4478 (1389) and 4480 (1400). Sotheby[3] gives a picture of a hand very like this one, from account books of The Hague, dated 1432, and notes 'it occurs frequently, during the fifteenth century, of different sizes'. It is thus likely that the paper came from Italy or, more probably, the Netherlands.

PRESENTATION, LAY-OUT, PUNCTUATION[4]

The MS. is devoid of decoration, and rubric initials are rare: they are used for the first letters of Nos. II, III, XIII, XIV, and XLIV (small letters are found beneath or beside many of these, indicating the letter to be written in red); a rubric initial at XIII. 229 marks a change of theme. The Epiphany hymn,

[1] C. M. Briquet, *Les Filigranes*, 4 vols. (Geneva, etc., 1907).

[2] V. A. Mošin and S. M. Traljić, *Vodeni Znakovi XIII i XIV Vijeka* (*Filigranes des XIIIᵉ et XIVᵉ siècles*), 2 vols. (Zagreb, 1957).

[3] S. L. Sotheby, *Principia Typographica*, 3 vols. (1858), vol. iii, *Paper-marks*, p. 8.

[4] For a full account of the layout, punctuation, capitalization, rubrics, and corrections, see thesis, i. xii–xvii.

No. xviii, has several rubric initials and small red marks in the
initial letters of some lines (see Appendix I, below, p. 119).

Almost all the verse items are laid out as verse, with a majuscule initial for each line: the exceptions, written as prose, are
Nos. xviii (second half), xli (no capitals), xlii and 21. Throughout the MS. rhymes in both English and Latin verse are marked
by thin lines in the margin, with only a few exceptions: the
system of marking rhymes varies according to the type of stanza
involved. The punctuation is very simple. The common para-
graph mark which resembles a suprascript a^1 is often found in
the left-hand margin; it is used to introduce new entries,
stanzas, and sections in a narrative, and to separate items in
lists. A symbol which consists of three dots with a tail shaped
like a figure 7 is sometimes found at the end of a text, after a
colophon or title, and once or twice concluding a section within
a narrative; in No. 21 it is used after stanzas, but it is nowhere
common. The symbol consisting of a dot and an oblique squiggle
above (somewhat resembling a *punctus medialis*) is used for both
exclamation and interrogation, but it is very rare. Words split
between lines are hyphenated with double oblique lines. Points
followed by one, two, or three oblique strokes are used (most
often in prose) to indicate pauses of varying length. Corrected
words are crossed through or expunged by subscript dots;
omitted words or lines are usually placed in the margin or at
the foot of the page or over the line, sometimes with a *caret* mark
in the text. Lines in the wrong order are marked with *b* and *a*
(to indicate that *a* should be placed immediately before *b*);
many corrections have been made throughout the text by
hand **A**.

Except at the beginning of verse lines, the use of capitals is
very haphazard: proper names appear with both minuscule and
majuscule initials (capitals are slightly more common for proper
names in English than in Latin). Capitals are sometimes used
at the beginning of English or Latin prose sentences, but with-

---

[1] C. Johnson and H. Jenkinson, *English Court Hand 1066 to 1500*, 2 vols.
(1915), i. 77; the mark was originally a majuscule *C* for *Capitulum*.

out any regularity or system. In English many minor words may have capital initials in the middle of sentences for no apparent reason; this is particularly true of *A* and *J*, which seem not to have been regarded as capital letters at all.

ORDER OF ENTRIES

The main text of ff. 1ᵇ–86ᵃ was almost certainly written by the same person. Although the handwriting changes often, the changes are usually gradual: it is hardly surprising that many items begin much more neatly than they end, or that some are written more carefully than others, or that the Latin rhythmical verse (where each line has the same number of syllables) is laid out more neatly than prose or English verse. Abrupt changes in the nature of the script may be due to: a fresher ink after a new dipping (e.g. f. 3ᵇ), a thinner nib after sharpening a worn one (ff. 21ᵃ, 27ᵃ, 68ᵃ), a change of pen (f. 28ᵇ), or simply tiredness (ff. 28ᵃ–28ᵇ, and the end of the MS.). The ink varies from light brown to a very dark grey: abrupt changes in the colour of ink from one item to the next probably indicate a lapse of time between entries (e.g. ff. 28ᵇ, 39ᵇ).

The number of lines per page varies greatly, between 40 and 55, usually about 45. There is no ruling on the paper at all.

T began to use the MS. as an account book (No. 1, f. 1ᵇ), but some time later abandoned this intention and used the rest of it for literary material. From f. 2ᵃ to f. 86ᵃ the entries are usually consecutive, but from changes in ink and nib it can be seen that some 'fill-ins' have been added later than the main entries on a page: recipe No. 1 (f. 1ᵇ) was written at the same time as No. 2 (f. 16ᵇ), which is probably contemporary with the other writing on f. 16ᵇ; the Easter poem, No. 20 (f. 58ᵇ), was probably written at the same time as the poems on Gaveston, Nos. XLI–XLII (ff. 63ᵃ–63ᵇ); the rules of conventual diet, No. XLIX (f. 76ᵇ), the pardon, No. LI (f. 78ᵇ), and the allegory of the cloister, No. LV (f. 85ᵇ), were probably all written at the same time.

The writing of six later hands can be seen in the MS.; these are referred to as hands **X, D, A, B, E**, and **C**. Hand **X** (late xv c.) filled in f. 1ª, f. 88ᵇ, and about half of f. 89ᵇ, all left blank by **T**, with four items (Appendix II, *1–*4): **X** must precede **A** because No. *19 by **A** is written after entries by **X** on f. 89ᵇ.

Hand **D** (early xvi c.) has written in titles to eight English and three Latin poems; **D** must precede **A**, as the latter has added *et earum contentio* after the title by **D** on f. 45ª (No. XXI).

Very extensive additions were made by hand **A** in the early years of Elizabeth's reign: several of them are dated, the latest being 4 June 1561 (No. *14). The entries first of all filled in the blank pages ff. 86ᵇ to 87ᵇ, and were then made as 'fill-ins' in spaces left by **T** and by hand **A** itself at the foot of pages near the end of the MS. (Appendix II, *5–*19). **A** also went through the whole of **T**'s entries closely, adding titles, page-headings, marginal notes, and even textual emendations (see Appendix I, No. x, below, p. 117, and thesis, ii. 195, 196); the writer of **A** was clearly a very learned man—he may be referred to in the damaged note No. *11 as Sowdene or John Pydsloy (however, see also below, p. 140, n. 2). The additions by **A** were made before the Twyne extracts of 1634.

A sloping, almost humanistic, hand **B** has added one or two more page-headings, following the lead set by **A**, completed the emendation to II. 216 begun by **A**, and written in five proverbs (*20) at appropriate places (f. 9ª, f. 28ᵇ, and three with **T**'s proverbs on f. 63ᵇ). Entries by **B** were also made before Twyne's extracts of 1634.

Hand **E** has only one or two notes: one on f. 2ª reads 'Bib. Cott. Vesp. E xii', another MS. of the 'Apocalypsis Goliæ'; it is possible that hand **E** is that of one of the scholars who examined the MS. (though it is not that of Hearne, and not very similar to the hands of James or Twyne).

Hand **C** has made one or two page-headings and titles, and the contents list on the inside of the vellum folder is also by

C (this list runs from No. II to No. XLIX, omitting all the small items and one or two important ones). Hand **C** is almost certainly that of Roger Gale himself,[1] as Hearne supposed;[2] on f.1ᵃ is written the number *E. 23*, a Gale shelf-mark.

There are also several marks and notes of doubtful authorship: see thesis, vol. i, xix–xx.

RECENT HISTORY[3]

(i) In or after 1628 Richard James, librarian of the Cotton collection, made several extracts from this MS.[4] There can be no doubt whatsoever that he was copying from **T**, but he twice refers to it as 'MS. Cotton'.

(ii) In or after 1634 the Oxford antiquarian Brian Twyne, Keeper of Archives (1634–44), made several very lengthy extracts from the MS.,[5] including the whole of xxviii (Tryvytlam) and several pieces of historical importance; it is through Twyne that the text of *13 (Sir Richard Gresham) can be restored, but it is clear that even in Twyne's time the MS. was damaged, as the ends of lines in *13 were not always visible to him. He also copied *20, the proverbs by **B**. Twyne refers to the MS. as being 'in Biblioth. D. Rob. Cotton' and describes

---

[1] The best examples of Gale's less formal handwriting are to be seen in MS. Rawlinson letters 6, Nos. 1–43; these resemble hand C closely. There is a good example of his formal writing in T.C.C. O.11.29, his letter donating the contents of his library to Trinity College.

[2] *Diary*, 1 June 1729, '. . . Dr. Gale in his table of contents at the beginning of the MS.' These words are omitted from the edition of the *Collections*: see below, p. 8, n. 2.

[3] For a full account of the handling of the MS. and of the transcription of some of the items by Richard James, Twyne, Gale, and Hearne, see thesis, i. xx–xxii.

[4] Bodley MS. James 7, pp. 84–8; an entry on p. 88 confirms the date 'in or after 1628'. The extracts include xv and xxx in full, short passages from III, VIII, XLII, and L, and quite lengthy excerpts from xxviii (Tryvytlam) and xxxi (the reply to Tryvytlam).

[5] Bodley MS. Twyne xxiv, pp. 299–307, dated in or after 1634 by an entry on p. 460. There is a brief description of the Twyne MS. by A. Clark, *Life and Times of Anthony Wood*, vol. iv (OHS xxx, 1895), 216. Anthony Wood himself seems to have known of **T** only through the extracts made by Twyne: he refers to it in Bodley MSS. Wood E. 4, p. 207, and Wood D. 18, pt. I, p. 39; thus, his description 'lib. MS. bib. Cott.' does not show that it was still in the Cotton collection in Wood's lifetime.

it as 'a narrow longe paper booke in a hand of K. Henry ye 6 time'. He was presumably lent the MS. by Richard James, but may not have returned it, for we next hear of it in the possession of Roger Gale.

(iii) In an unprinted letter to Hearne, dated 22 February 1729,[1] Gale described the MS. as 'a Miscellaneous Collection of severall pieces in prose and verse, Latin and English . . . The book seems to have belonged to Glastonbury abbey, tho' some things have been entred in it, in the reign of Queen Elizabeth.' Gale's main interest seems to have been in xxvIII, of which he transcribed lines 1–12 and sent them to Hearne.

(iv) In his *Diary* for 1729[2] Hearne referred to the MS. three times, on 13 April, 10 May, and 1 June; he was lent the MS. by Gale on 5 April. On 1 June he made his own contents list and transcribed five items in full; he later printed the whole of Tryvytlam's poem, No. xxvIII,[3] and referred to the MS. as *semilacero et squallore obsito codice Galeano*. Hearne returned the MS. to Gale in time for it to be included in the donation of Gale's library to Trinity College on 21 July 1738.

It may be useful to summarize the history of the MS. briefly: in the middle of the fifteenth century a Glastonbury monk began to use it as an account book, but subsequently filled it with literary material; soon afterwards hand **X** filled in some blank spaces, and hand **D** supplied several titles. In 1539 (before or after hand **D**) Glastonbury Abbey was dissolved. Some time later, after the accession of Elizabeth (November 1558) hand **A** filled in the remaining blank pages, and annotated the text of **T**: his last entry was made after 1561. Shortly after this the MS. was allowed to get very damp, and its condition

---

[1] MS. Rawlinson letters 6, No. 40.

[2] This period of Hearne's diary is edited by H. E. Salter, *Remarks and Collections of Thomas Hearne*, vol. x (OHS lxvii, 1915), particularly pp. 119, 129, 136–41; the original text, Bodley MS. Hearne's diaries, 121 (pp. 22, 48, 68–83), contains some interesting details omitted in Salter's edition: cf. p. 7, n. 2, and Appendix I, p. 138. The items transcribed by Hearne were Nos. 3, xLI, xLII, L, and Appendix II, No. *6.

[3] T. Hearne (ed.), *Historia Vitæ et Regni Ricardi II* (1729), Appendix, pp. 344–58, and Preface, p. xvii.

began to deteriorate. Somehow it passed into the Cotton library, where it was examined by Richard James, who also lent it to Brian Twyne in Oxford. During the next hundred years it somehow became the property of Roger Gale, who examined it and made a contents list on its cover (and probably had it bound in its present binding); Gale also lent it to Thomas Hearne, who made a thorough analysis of it. In 1738 it went to Trinity College, Cambridge, where it probably first acquired the pencil foliation.

DATE AND PROVENANCE

The date traditionally given to the MS., 'about 1450', is fully justified by the evidence. Three items are dated in the fifteenth century: No. 3 (Henry VI's entry into Paris) was written in December 1431; No. XLIV (Bruni's translation of the story of Tancred) was translated in 1436 or 1438;[1] No. L (Nicholas Frome's letter: Appendix I, below, pp. 130–9) was written in Cologne on 9 June 1434. Many other items can be given fairly precise dates, often in the fourteenth century. The handwriting is typical of the middle of the fifteenth century.

The Glastonbury associations of the MS. are overwhelming: in Appendix I are printed several items which demonstrate this, including the list of assessments on abbey holdings, two poems honouring the legendary founder of the abbey, Joseph of Arimathea, a note by Abbot Henry de Blois, and a text of Nicholas's letter which was specifically addressed to two monks of Glastonbury, John Ledbury and Richard Busard.[2] In the Appendix it is also suggested that other items may owe their inclusion to associations with Glastonbury. Also printed in the Appendix is a poem with the title 'Ingratitudo' (not found elsewhere) composed by Stephen Deverell, monk of the abbey.[3]

---

[1] Both dates are given in texts of a letter from Bruni; see below, p. 90.

[2] These names were fully visible only to Richard James; neither of them appears in the list of monks present at the election of Abbot Walter More in 1456; the list is printed by T. B. Snow, 'Glastonbury', *Downside Review*, ix (1890), 186–212, particularly p. 200.

[3] The date of composition of this poem is unknown. Deverell's name does not appear in the list of 1456 (n. 2 ,above), nor in earlier lists such as that

On the whole the scribe's orthography is conservative: the
sounds indicated by the spellings are basically those of the late
fourteenth century, and the spellings are similar to those one
might expect to find in a MS. of Chaucer. Although the text
is clearly localized at Glastonbury, there are few south-western
dialect characteristics. The consistency of the orthography,
despite the fact that the scribe was dealing with texts from
several different areas, indicates a high degree of literacy:[2] the
scribe may have studied at Oxford (Glastonbury had close links
with Gloucester College) or London, or may have been excep-
tionally well read in the literary products of the court. The
present description necessarily tends to emphasize dispropor-
tionately the abnormal features of the language; it is on the
rare features of the orthography that reflect fifteenth-century
changes in pronunciation that the first section, on phonology,
concentrates. The morphology is such as one would expect of
a southern English text of this date: there are a few 'modern'
features.

(i) *Phonology*

In words with ME variation between /a/ and /ɔ(:)/ before
nd, *ng*, the spelling is normally *o*, but a few *a* forms occur
(as in *hand-* beside *honde*). Late ME raising of /e/ > /i/ before
nasals is seen often, in *thynke, yngke, crymsyn, Ingelond, Imperes*

printed by F. A. Gasquet, 'List of Glastonbury monks . . . in A.D. 1377',
Downside Review, xi (1892), 150–1, or in the Indexes to *The Great Chartulary
of Glastonbury Abbey* (compiled *c.* 1338–40), ed. Dom A. Watkin, *Somerset
Record Society*, lix, lxiii, lxiv (1947–56).
    [1] In this section only the most significant features of the language are
mentioned; for a full description of the phonology (stressed and unstressed
vowels, and consonants), morphology, and syntax, see thesis, i. xxiv–lxxvi:
pp. xxv–xlvii 'Phonology', pp. xlviii–liv 'Morphology', pp. liv–lxxvi 'Syntax'. In this present description a 'broad' phonetic transcription has been
used. The thesis also includes an analysis of the language of the Latin contents (phonology only), i. lxxvi–lxxxii.
    [2] An exception to the general consistency of orthography and morphology
is No. 4, 'The Feat of Gardeninge', edited in Appendix I, below pp. 103–
16. See also thesis, ii. 238–9, and *N. & Q.* ccxi (1966), 324–30.

(beside some *e* forms); most of the other examples of *y* (/i/) for ME /e/ can be explained by late OE variations, but *tyxte* 'text' may show simple raising.[1] Lengthening of /e/>/ɛː/ in open syllables is confirmed by several rhymes, but the spelling *ettyth* 'eats' may indicate a failure to lengthen in the pr. 3 sg. The conservative nature of the spelling is shown by the fact that although lowering of /er/>/ar/ had almost certainly taken place, the spelling of words with this sound is usually *er*: that lowering has taken place is indicated by a few back-spellings of ME /ar/ (OE *ear*) by *er* (*sperhawke, scherpnysse, dere*, 'I dare').[2]

Lengthening of /i/>/eː/ in open syllables is probably shown by *e* spellings in *leue* 'live' (the only spelling in the text), *smete* 'smitten', *wete* 'know', etc. Some of these *e* spellings could also show OE variation in words with velar umlaut of /i/>/eo/; they could also show lowering of /i/>/e/ (cf. *wemmen* 'women', twice, which certainly has a short vowel)—the vowel is probably also short in *preuely, velany, infenyte*.[3]

In words which show ME *i, u,* or *e* from OE *y*, the spelling is normally *y* (/i/), but *e* is also found (e.g. *lefte, mery, steryth, cleche*, and, with lengthening, *meynde* 'mind' n.), and less often *u* (*kutte, ysturyd, frust*). It should be noted that while some poems have rhymes which confirm both /i/ and /e/, none of them confirms /u/; this may suggest that the scribe sometimes introduced his own dialectal /u/ into the text, but the poems are too brief for any conclusive inference to be made. Most variations from /i/ are those which have survived in Standard English (*left, merry,* etc.).

Lengthening of /o/>/ɔː/ in open syllables and before consonant groups is often shown by spellings with *oo* and confirmed by rhymes. ME /u/ normally appears with *u* or *o* (to avoid minim confusion), but the second *o* of *honysoke* may show lengthening of /u/>/ɔː/ (for the corresponding shortening, see below): the raising of this /oː/>/uː/ may be seen in *dowfes*, 'doves', which

---

[1] Dobson § 77 (a) (v).

[2] These spellings are regarded as phonetically significant by Luick, 364 A. 3, but Kihlbom, p. 121, with more probability takes them as back-spellings. [3] For lowering of /i/>/e/, see Dobson § 80.

cannot simply be lengthening of ME /u/ which was always to /o:/.[1]

The MS. naturally makes no distinction in spelling between ME /e:/ and /ɛ:/, and rhymes in several poems clearly show that /ɛ:/ has been raised to /e:/—nowhere are they kept apart in rhyme. Both ME /ɛ:/ and /e:/ occasionally appear spelt *y*. Such spellings admit of various explanations: some may show OE (WS) *īe*, *ȳ* (e.g. *hyre* 'hear', *lyueȝt* 'believes', and, by analogy, *bylyue* 'belief', etc.); they may also show shortening of ME /e:/>/i/[2] (*fyll* 'fell' (v.) is certainly such a case); finally, they may show the raising of /e:/>/i:/.[3] No explanation satisfies all the cases, but it is in any case best not to adduce south-western dialectal differences to explain such forms as *hyre* 'hear', *schyne* 'bright', etc., in view of the widespread extent of such spellings in late ME. Rhymes involving ME /ɛ:/ and /e:/ never confirm either raising or shortening: for instance, *grene*: *schyne* may show /e:/ or /i:/ or /i/.

The converse of this problem is seen in words spelt with *e* for ME /i:/ (e.g. *streke* 'strike', *lekyng* 'pleasure' and cognate words, *bygelyd* 'beguiled'). According to Dobson,[4] the words with *k* show shortening of ME /i:/>/i/, and subsequent lengthening of /i/>/e:/ in open syllables.

A few rhymes show ME /ɔ:/>/o:/, but normally it may be assumed that the two sounds are distinct. One southern dialect feature of poem No. 4, obscured by the spelling, is the rhyme *pympernold*: *wold* ('the plant weld'), 179–80—as *pimpernel* normally has the -*el* suffix, it is probable that *wold* shows /ɛ:/ or /e:/ from OE (non-Anglian) *weald*, and that the scribe has not noticed this exclusively southern dialect feature.

Raising of ME /o:/>/u:/ is shown by the spelling *smowth* 'smooth' (in this MS. *ow* is a graph for ME /u:/ and /oṷ/ only)—cp. also *dowfes* discussed above. Shortening of /o:/>/u/ is seen in the verb *muste* beside *moste*.

[1] See E. J. Dobson, 'Middle English lengthening in open syllables', *Transactions of the Philological Society* (1962), 124–48.
[2] Dobson §§ 116 n. 2, 122, and 132 n.
[3] Dobson § 136 n. 2.   [4] § 138.2.

No distinction is made in spelling between early ME /ei/ and /ai/, both of which may be assumed to have /æi/ at this time; late ME monophthongization to /a:/ (or /a/) is shown by the spelling *mastrees* 'mistress'; at the end of No. 4 the scribe has crossed through *mas* before writing *mayster*. The 'sporadic dialectal' development of ME /eg/ > /ig/ > /i:/ is shown once in a rhyme from No. 4, *wyde*: *leyde* 33–4.[1] One set of rhymes indicates the development of /oụ/ > /aụ/,[2] *thowȝt*: *ywroȝt*: *ytawȝtte*: *noȝt*. The pronunciation of ME /oụ/ as /u:/[3] is shown in the rhyme *prow*: *ystrow* 4. 85–6, and is probably demonstrated conclusively[4] by *grownde* : *growynde* 'growing' 4. 57–8 (in which *grownde* must have ME /u:/ lengthened from OE /u/). There is nothing to show whether spellings in *ow*, *ou*, for ME /o:/ before *g*, *h*, indicate /o:ụ/ or /u:ụ/; the spelling *deuoȝte* 'devout' is a back-spelling indicating /oht/ > /u:t/ (for the use of *ȝ* to show length, see below). There is no need to assume a failure to diphthongize in spellings such as *ywroȝt*, *broght*: graphs such as *oght* are to be regarded as spellings representing the diphthong. On the other hand, *softe* 'sought' and *nofte* 'nothing' do not have a diphthong.

Among the vowels not bearing the main stress can be seen the raising of /e/ > /i/: spellings in *-es*, *-ys*, *-ed*, *-yd*, etc., occur in about equal proportion. The reduction of pretonic /a/ > /ə/ is indicated by some spelling confusion, particularly in the use of *a* for other non-stressed vowels.

Only the most interesting and significant of the consonant developments can be mentioned here.[5] Weakening of final /ŋg/ > /ŋ/, or even /n/, is shown by a few rhymes (notably in No. 4), but by no spellings: T in fact often emphasizes the velar quality of /ŋg/ by using *ngg*, even in etymologically final position. On the other hand, both rhymes and spellings show a weakening of final /nd/ > /n/—particularly back-spellings such as *onde* 'one' 4. 158: most examples of this are found in No. 4,

---

[1] Dobson § 137 n. 2 (c). [2] Dobson §§ 89 and 240.
[3] Dobson § 173 and n. 1.
[4] Against the view of Jordan § 280.
[5] A full account of the consonants is given in thesis, i. xli–xlviii.

but *an* 'and' is found once elsewhere. After French /au/ and ME /uː/ (spelt *ou* or *ouw*), the letter *n* is often omitted (e.g. *fouwde* 'found', *marchawtys* 'merchants', etc.); this omission (also seen in some of the Paston Letters and in the Brome MS.) is purely graphic and can have no phonetic significance.

Variation between /d/ and /ð/ before /ʀ/ is common (e.g. *feder*, *fether*). In some words voiceless /f/ appears to have been transferred into parts of words, i.e. intervocalically, where OE had /v/ (e.g. *wyffes*); however, *ff* here may simply be a graph for /v/. Similarly, *dowffes*, which had /v/ in both singular and plural in OE, may show the spread of /f/ after the loss of final *-e*.[1]

Unvoicing of final /nd/>/nt/ (particularly noticeable when caused by the late ME loss of final *-e*) is often of morphological significance, distinguishing the present and preterite of some verbs; it is seen in such rhymes as *ywente* pt. pp.: *schente* pt. pp.: *entente*, but there are also other rhymes which indicate /nd/ in similar circumstances. The voiceless quality of final /s/ in unstressed words is confirmed by occasional spellings in *ss(e)*, and by the rhyme *face*: *wasse* 'was'.

Vocalization of /x/ before /t/, and consequent lengthening of the preceding vowel, are indicated by back-spellings: *whyȝte* 'white', *condyȝt* 'conduit', *abouȝt*, etc. On the other hand, not all such unetymological *ght*, *ȝt*, spellings indicate a preceding long vowel.[2] There is great variety in the spellings of ME /ht/ (*ght*, *gth*, *th*, *ȝt*, *ȝth*), and these spellings have been extended to words which did not have final *t* (e.g. *thought* 'though', *thowght* 'tough'), and even to the ending of the present 3rd sg. in which *-yȝth*, *-yȝt*, *-eȝth*, *-eȝt*, often appear for *-(y)th*: in these last occurrences there can be no question of a long vowel. The development of /xt/>/ft/[3] is seen twice, in *softe* 'sought' and *nofte* 'nothing'.

Vocalization of /l/ is seen in *herbe Water* 'herb Walter' 4. 164;[4]

---

[1] Cf. Jordan § 217; such unvoicing is often regarded as purely northern.
[2] As argued with reference to *Sir Launfal* by A. J. Bliss, *Anglia*, lxxv, N.S., lxi (1957), 275–89.
[3] Jordan § 196 A., Dobson § 371.
[4] Dobson § 425.

loss of /d/ is common in the word *worl(l)e* beside *worlde*. The development of /hw/>/ʍ/ or /w/ is seen in spellings such as *wyche*, and in back-spellings *wharre* 'war', *where* 'were'. Loss of /w/[1] before ME /ɔ:/ (perhaps raised to /o:/) is seen in *hoo* 'who' frequently (nominative only) beside *who*, *too* beside *two(o)*, *soote* 'sweat', *forsoore* 'forsworn'; before /u:/ in *forsownyng* 'swooning' beside *swonyng*;[2] and after /o:/ in *foore* 'four' beside (normal) *fowre*. Loss of initial /h/ is found in weakly stressed words, such as *it*, and in *eruyst* 'harvest'.

Initial and medial /v/ is often spelt *w*: *waryabyll*, *knawe* 'boy', *schawe* 'shave', *velewette*.[3] The rhyme *cloth* : *loffe* 'loaf' is perhaps an instance of dialectal final /þ/>/f/.[4] The spelling *bagbytyng* 'back-biting' (recorded in the *OED* and *MED*) perhaps shows a development of /k/>/g/ before /b/.[5]

(ii) *Morphology*

There is little of note in the declension of the nouns: there are one or two survivals of 'uninflected' genitives; the pronominal substitution for the genitive is seen once only, in *Sampson hys story* (in fact an error for *Susannys*); -*s* is found as a genitive and plural inflexion (as well as -*es*, -*ys*) after consonants as well as vowels. The only surviving weak *n*-plural is in *yen* 'eyes', but -*en* has been extended to an OE strong feminine noun in *fetheren* beside *fedyrs* (the *n*-plural is also recorded in *MED*).

In the 3rd person plural pronoun, the nominative always has *th*- (except *hy* once, 4. 83); the accusative and dative have 30 *h* forms (*ham*, *hem*) of which 20 are in No. 4, and 13 *th* (*them*,

---

[1] Dobson §§ 420, 421.

[2] OE *geswógen* produces both /u:/ and /o:/ in ME. However, the evidence of other texts suggests that *forsownyng* (9.2: see below, p. 54) means not 'swooning' but 'sighing': I owe this suggestion to Mrs. Autumn Simmons of Stanford.

[3] For the significance of such spellings, see Jordan § 300.

[4] Dobson § 374. This occurrence antedates the example from *The Book of Quint Essence*, cited by H. C. Wyld, *History of Modern Colloquial English*, 3rd edn. (1953), p. 291.

[5] A stone sign near Horwich, Lancashire, has BLAGBURN for Blackburn.

tham, theym, thaym); genitive, 18 *h* (*her, here, hare*), 2 in No. 4, 24 *th* (*theyr, theyre, ther*(*e*), *thayr*). No. 4 has only *h-* forms in the oblique cases, which confuses the statistical significance of the distribution; it seems that **T** was accustomed to use *th* forms only in the nominative, but both (with a slight preference for *th*) in the oblique cases. The plural of the demonstrative pronoun *thys* (once *thes*) is usually *thys, this,* but *thes*(*e*) also occurs.

The normal pr. 3 sg. ending of verbs was clearly *-(y)th*, etc.: only once is *-ys* found (*settisse* in No. 23) outside poem No. 5, in which both *-yth* and *-ys* endings are found side by side. **T** has in fact altered an *-s* ending against the rhyme in *seyth* : *peese*, and was thus clearly only accustomed to *-th*. The pr. 3 pl. varies between *-(y)th*, etc., and no ending (*-e*) in about equal proportion, often in the same piece; *-en* occurs once only.

For the unvoicing of final /nd/>/nt/ in the preterite of weak verbs, see above p. 14. In strong verbs there are several examples of the transference of the vowel of the pt. sg. to the plural, and vice versa; this is as expected, and there are no cases which are not fully evidenced from other texts. Final *-n* in the pt. pp. is not common either in the spelling of **T**, or in the rhymes of any of the poems, except in Lydgate's No. 11, where **T** has often omitted the *-n* against the rhyme: **T** never adds *-n* against the rhyme, and one may conclude that it was not part of his language. The *y-* prefix is rare in the MS.: it does not occur in twelve items; it is common in No. 4, and otherwise occurs sporadically, in no fixed pattern.

Final *-n* is rare in the infinitive, and is confined to verbs of native origin; it is seen mainly in No. 4, where it is often confirmed by rhyme (as it is once or twice elsewhere). Its absence is also often confirmed by rhyme, even in No. 4. A number of verbs have infinitives in *-y*(*ne*), e.g. *swery, graffy, flatery, rypyne,* etc.; these may indicate a dialectal preference for *-y* as an infinitive ending, but many of them can be explained in different ways.

The present participle is always in *-yng*, but *growynde*

'growing', 4. 58, a verbal noun, has adopted the *-inde* ending of the Southern ME present participle.

May has pr. 2 sg. in both *my3t*, etc., and *mayste*. *Schall* usually has pr. pl. in *schall*, but *ye schul* is found once, 4. 101. The present forms of *will* vary considerably (*woll, wull, wyll*; the negative form is *nell*, pr. 1 sg.).

(iii) *Syntax*

The plural of polite address (*ye, yow*) is found unequivocally only once, in *wene ye that y loue hym?* (wife to husband), though it occurs several times in the Latin story, No. XVII. There are many poems in which the poet addresses the audience in both singular and plural, which suggests that the plural form does not necessarily imply more than one person.

The use of *hyt* as a formal anticipatory or resumptive subject is very common in sentences such as *to lete hym grow to hye hit ys grete foly*, 4. 135, but there are also some cases (mainly in No. 4) where *hyt* is omitted in positions where PrE would require it, e.g. *yn what moneth ys best ham sette and sow*, 4. 151.

The most common relative pronoun is *that*, but also found are *(the) wych(e)* and *whos* (genitive—the nominative *who* never occurs as a relative pronoun). There are two instances of the omission of the subject relative pronoun; both follow *ther(e)+* the verb 'to be', e.g. *som ther byth woll be*; in the following sentence either the subject relative or the personal pronoun has been omitted: *hyt is not by them that y ment, But by small damsellys and tender of age, Wyth ther mysgouernawce makyth wyves to be schent*. The object relative pronoun is never omitted. In 'whoever, whatever' clauses, *hoo, who, what*, etc., are followed by *that*, or by *so* or *ever*, or by both *so* and *ever*.

The negative particle *not* (etc.) is usually placed after the finite verb, after the object pron., or after the subject pron. if the subject and verb are reversed; only once is it found before the verb: *owre feyth no3t halte3th* (confirmed by other MSS.). There is no occurrence of the auxiliary verb *do* to form a negative. Multiple negatives are very common, particularly in 'neither . . . nor' sentences.

Introductory *ther(e)* is very commonly used; in existential statements, in sentences where the emphasis is on the predicate or on a dependent clause, in sentences where the subject is long and therefore placed after the verb, and in order to provide a formal 'subject' for a passive verb (e.g. *ther was made an hegge*), though forms without *there* also occur (e.g. *and atte the comyng yn atte gate was ordeynd a clothe*).

There is no example of the durative use of *be*+pr. pp., but the pr. pp. is often loosely attached to the main verb. There are several examples of pleonastic *do*, often with consuetudinal force (*the deuell wyth kyssyng meny on doth wynne*), or to form a simple preterite. The verb *do* never means 'cause' in this text (*let* or *make* is used). There are several examples of 'consuetudinal' *will* (in the 'boys will be boys' sense), e.g. *thys wykkyd world woll haue hys wone*.

The uses of the subjunctive, conditional sentences, modal auxiliaries such as *should, would, might*, are all extremely complex; there is nothing particularly striking about their uses in this text, but a full analysis is given in thesis, vol. i. lxx–lxxiv.

ORIGIN OF THE CONTENTS

(i) *Items unique to this manuscript*

Under this heading are all the 'Glastonbury items' (Nos. I, X, XIX–XX, XXVI, XLIX, and L), English Nos. 1, 2, 10, 15, 18, and (in its present form) 23, and Latin Nos. VI, IX, XIII, XIV, XVII, XVIII, XXI, XXIII, XXVIII–XXXI, XXXII, XXXVII, XLI–XLII, XLVIII, LI, and LVI–LVII. It is necessary to consider whether any of these (excluding No. 1, the accounts) may have been the original compositions of the scribe himself. Also to be considered here are some items which are longer in **T** than elsewhere, and which may owe their new form to this scribe: No. VIII (the longest version of the ungrammatical 'Satyricum in abbates', xxxiii (the expanded version of the 'Descriptio Northfolchiæ'), and xxxix (a longer version of the poem on 'Fortune').

Two kinds of evidence can be used—external and textual. No. ix, 'Stores of the Cities', can probably be dated before 1401 and is unlikely to be by T; xiii is almost certainly by the thirteenth-century canon, Walter of Wimborne; xxviii and xxix, both written by friars, are fourteenth-century poems; similarly, xxxi is probably a contemporary reply to xxviii, written c. 1360 (the only alternative date is c. 1320); xli–xlii, poems celebrating the death of Piers Gaveston, were written shortly after his execution, certainly before 1322 and probably before 1314; xlviii 'St. Hilda and Whitby Abbey' is known to have existed in another MS. localized in the eighteenth century near the probable place of composition; xlix 'Conventual diet' by Abbot Henry de Blois was probably taken from some Glastonbury history or document; l is a copy of a letter sent from Cologne by Nicholas Frome, Abbot of Glastonbury. A large number of unique items are shown by textual errors to be copies from other MSS.: these include English Nos. 10, 'Hyre and see', and 18, 'What euer thow sey', in which the scribe has incorporated the word *loke* into the text against the rhymé, probably from a marginal gloss. Of the Latin items the following have scribal errors which suggest that T was copying from elsewhere: Nos. vi, 'Gregory's Garden', x, 'Epitaph of Joseph of Arimathea', xvii, 'Wager Story' (some of the errors in this story may be due to the adaptation from an earlier version), xviii, 'Epiphany hymn' (from the lay-out it seems that the scribe thought of the hymn as two separate pieces), xxi, 'Debate between Winter and Summer' (this has errors, and is also incomplete), xxvi, 'Ingratitudo' by Stephen Deverell (without the errors we could not be sure that Stephen and the scribe T were not the same person), and li, a pardon (some letters have been inserted above the line). The fact that T (erroneously) attributes xxxiii, 'Non-celebrant priests', to Bede indicates that he did not compose it himself.

T can hardly be said to have 'composed' the accounts list

No. 1, and, although No. 23 (proverbs) is a unique arrangement, almost all the proverbs are found separately elsewhere. After these eliminations we are left with Nos. 1 and 2 (medical recipes), 15 (macaronic poem on death), xiv, 'De cantu Alma Redemptoris Mater' (the miracle of the boy of Toledo, which exists in other versions), xix–xx (hymn and prayer to the two St. Josephs), xxiii, 'Felix qui poterit' (proverb), xxx, 'De astantibus crucifixo' (story against the friars), xxxvii (interpretation of the name *William*), lv (an allegory of the cloister), and lvi–lvii (hymn and prayer to St. Uritha—this text is too damaged to detect any scribal errors, but may perhaps safely be assumed to come from Devon, the home of the saint). All of these, then, *may* have been composed by **T**, but it should be stated firmly that there is no positive evidence for his authorship, and in most cases probability is against it.

In No. viii, the 'Satyricum in abbates' in bad Latin, it is impossible to tell if there are any errors in the sections unique to **T**; the two additional stories in xxxiii, 'Descriptio Northfolchiæ', 44–97 and 200–25, are not found elsewhere, but errors in the second indicate that they are not to be ascribed to **T**. No. xxxix, 'Fortune', has two lines (5–6) not found elsewhere; it is doubtful if they are to be credited to **T**. On the other hand it is probable that we have **T** to thank for the prose lines which introduce the verses in xi, 'Luxuria', and for the rewriting of No. 12 (originally in rhyme royal) with the ballade-stanza *ababbcbc*.

(ii) *Items found in other texts*

All the remaining items are found in other MSS. The English contents, in order of popularity, are: No. 20, 'How to find the date of Easter' (15 MSS.);[1] No. 11, Lydgate's 'Ram's Horn' (9 MSS.); No. 8, 'Parce michi domine' (7 MSS.); No. 9, 'Ever thank God' (6 MSS.); No. 17, 'Wyth thys bytel' (5 MSS.); No. 12 'Beware the blynde', probably also by Lydgate (3 MSS.

---

[1] Numbers of MSS. in parentheses in this section are all *excluding* **T**.

and an edition by Stow from one of the extant texts); No. 19, 'Conditions of a good horse' (4 MSS.); No. 3, 'Coronation of Henry VI' (3 MSS. of, or derived from, the London Chronicle); and Nos. 6, 'Revertere', 7, 'Who seyth sothe', and 13, 'Ho hath good' (2 MSS. each); the following are found in one other MS. only: Nos. 4, 'Feat of Gardeninge', 5, 'Pluk of here bellys', 16, 'Hoo that comy3t', 21, 'Who can not wepe', and 22, 'Beware of sweryng'. We can usually infer from the types of error common in these texts (e.g. transposition of lines, omissions by haplography, etc.), that **T** was copying from a *written* exemplar, but there is rarely any further indication of his source. No. 3 is almost certainly a copy of a letter, not now extant, sent from a Paris correspondent (cf. No. L, Nicholas Frome's letter, mentioned above); No. 20 is a mnemonic device to find the date of Easter, and may have been copied from a calendar or from memory. No. 16 is a verse also found in Bodley MS. 315 into which it was copied from some verses on the refectory wall of the Austin Priory at Launceston: it is possible that **T** had visited Launceston (about seventy-five miles from Glastonbury) and had remembered the verse, which is, however, only a fuller statement of a well-known proverb. No. 17 is a verse which concludes a well-known sermon exemplum, and may have been copied by **T** from a collection of Bromyard's sermons, or from a text of *Dives et Pauper*; on the other hand it is also found separately elsewhere. Apart from these speculations, we have no evidence of the origin of the English items: from a textual analysis of all of them it is clear that **T** did not copy from any extant MS., nor was **T** used by any surviving text as an exemplar.

Some of the Latin items were very popular indeed in the Middle Ages:[1] countless MS. texts survive of Nos. LII–LIV, the Histories of the True Cross, of Pilate, and of Judas Iscariot (the

---

[1] It is impractical in many cases to be any more specific than this: Walther's *Initia* is naturally imprecise about the number of MSS. of the very popular poems, and in some cases the same poem is listed more than once in different entries. There is no sure guide to the number of MSS. of some of the prose items, such as XLIV and LII–LIV.

last two were also given further popularity by their inclusion in the *Legenda Aurea* of Jacobus a Voragine); over 68 MSS. of No. II, 'Apocalypsis Goliæ', are recorded by its editor Strecker, and over 60 of No. III, 'De poena coniugii', are known to Walther. Other very popular long items include No. VIII, the burlesque 'Satyricum in abbates', No. VII, 'Debate between Water and Wine' (over 20 MSS.), and No. XXII, 'Tempus acceptabile', a call for repentance (over 10 MSS., English and foreign). Many of the short proverbial items (including drinking-songs and quasi-medical lore) were also extremely popular: it is impossible to regard Walther as a useful indication of the number of MSS., as the catalogues which he used rarely mention such small items. Of all the Latin contents of the MS. only a few could be edited critically with any confidence that the total number of extant MSS. was known: Nos. IV, 'De virtute clavium' (7 other MSS., including one seventeenth-century transcript), V, 'De quatuor raptoribus' (2 MSS.), XXIV, 'Death' (2 MSS.), and XXXIII, 'Descriptio Northfolchiæ' (5 MSS.).

We can speculate on the origin of only one or two of the Latin entries: No. XII (proverb) is from Peter Comestor's *Historia Scholastica*; No. XLVII, 'The soul in hell', was taken from John the Deacon's *Vita S. Gregorii*; No. XLIV, Leonardo Bruni's translation of Boccaccio's story of Guiscardo and Ghismonda, may have been taken from one of the first printed editions (1436 or 1438) of the translation, but the text is also found in other MSS. No. XXIV, 'Death', is found in two MSS. of the English treatise 'Disce mori', but it is probably to be regarded as a separate poem, not an integral part of the treatise. Apart from one or two proverbial items which may have been written down from memory, it is likely that all entries were copied from a written exemplar.

It is remarkable that out of eighty Latin and English items in the MS. not one can be shown to have been copied from, or been copied by, any MS. now extant: there is no positive evidence for such copying, and there are many cases where the evidence is definitely against it.[1] An illuminating illustration of this point can be seen in the case of MSS. which contain more than one of **T**'s entries: not one of these can be shown to have any direct connection with **T**, either as its source or as a copy made from **T**. The following well-known 'Goliardic' MSS. contain several items found in **T**: Cotton Titus A. xx (xiii c.) has Nos. II, III, IV, VII, and XXXIII, and its 'sister-manuscript' Rawlinson B. 214 (xv c.) has all these except VII; Corpus Christi College, Cambridge, MS. 481 (xiii c.) has Nos. II and IV; Trinity College, Cambridge, O.2.45 (after 1248) has II and XXXIII; Harley 978 (xiii c.) has II, III, V, and XXXIV. From my editions of Nos. IV, XXXIII, and XXXIV[2] it is clear that none of these MSS. has any direct connection with **T**. I have no evidence for or against a connection with Cotton Vespasian E. xii (Nos. II and III), Bodley 496 (II, III, VII, XXII), or Digby 166 (VII, XXII).

Similar arguments based on textual variants can be used to dispose of possible connections with the following MSS.: Simeon and Vernon MSS. (late xiv c., Nos. 7 and 9), Harley 2251 (xv c., a Shirley aureate collection, Nos. 11 and 12), Bannatyne MS. (1568, Nos. 11 and 13), Trinity College, Cambridge, R.3.19 (xv/xvi c., Nos. 12 and XXXIV), Lansdowne 762 (late xv c., Nos. 14 and 19), Book of St. Alban's (1486, Nos. 14 and 19), Harley 3362 (xvi c., Nos. IV in part, XXV, XXXIX, XL, XLVI, and Appendix II No. *20. iv), and Balliol 354 (Richard Hill's sixteenth-century commonplace book, which has Nos. 6, 20, 22, XVI, XXVI*a*, and XXXIV).[3] Several of the short quasi-medical pieces are also found in the *Regimen Sanitatis*[4] (xi/xii c., Nos. XXXIV and XLIII *b–c*) and in the two versions of the *Flos medicinæ*[5]

[1] See thesis i. xcvi–xcviii.

[2] Thesis, i. 2–7, 146–57, ii. 197–202, 356–72.

[3] A connection between **T** and Balliol 354 was hinted at (on the basis of No. 22 only) by R. L. Greene, 'The meaning of the Corpus Christi Carol', *M.Æ* xxix (1960), 14, and again in *SEC*, p. 231. However, see my remarks in *N. & Q.* ccxi (1966), 329–30.

[4] Sir A. Croke (ed.), *Regimen Sanitatis Salernitanum* (1830); this edition was based on the text printed in 1484 by Arnald of Villa Nova. The traditional ascription of the *Regimen* to John of Milan dates only from the fifteenth century. It is a short poem consisting mainly of well-known proverbs.

[5] The two arrangements were printed by S. de Renzi (ed.), *Collectio*

(part i has xxv, xxxiv, xl, xliii *b–c*, part ii all these except xxv): there is no suggestion that **T** derived his pieces from these medical works (for instance **T** has the older, short version of xxxiv), and they were in any case compiled largely from proverbs which circulated separately, as in **T**.

To summarize: although we can usually be sure that even items unique to **T** were not the composition of the scribe himself, and that he copied nearly every entry in the MS. from a written exemplar, nevertheless we have no extant text in which a direct connection with **T** can be demonstrated, and in the most telling cases, where MSS. contain more than one item also in **T**, we often have conclusive evidence against any such connection.

LITERARY INTEREST OF THE MANUSCRIPT

(i) *Commonplace Books*

This book belongs to the class of MSS. (found in increasing numbers in the late fifteenth and the sixteenth centuries) known as 'commonplace books'. Commonplace books are collections of miscellaneous material assembled simply for the interest and amusement of the compiler. The characteristics of this kind of book[1] are perhaps best described negatively. Song-books, such as MS. Sloane 2593, compiled by minstrels for professional purposes, are not included; nor are sermon source-books, such as that of the Franciscan John Grimestone, Advocates' MS. (National Library of Scotland) 18.7.21;[2] also excluded because of their singleness of purpose are personal devotional collections such as Harley 172, which contains a mixture of religious verse (including Lydgate and Hoccleve) and prose. On the

Salernitana, 5 vols. in 3 (Naples, 1852–9), i. 445–516; v. 1–104. The *Flos Medicinæ* is more systematic and less popular in tone than the earlier *Regimen*, most of which is incorporated into the *Flos Medicinæ*.

[1] The best account of the strictly defined concept of a commonplace book is by Robbins *SL*, Introduction, pp. xxviii–xxx. For the compilation of miscellanies in *scriptoria* for private citizens, see H. S. Bennett, 'Medieval English MSS. and contemporary taste', *Edinburgh Bibliographical Society Transactions*, ii (1938–45), 382–3.

[2] See i.a. Brown *RL XIV*, Introduction, pp. xvi–xix.

other hand a specifically religious interest is often found in commonplace books: for instance, Sloane 1584, the commonplace book of Canon John Gysborn,[1] has predominantly religious contents but also includes English medical recipes and a few secular poems. As the contents are purely individual and represent the taste of the compiler only, books produced in *scriptoria* are also excluded, no matter how catholic the miscellany (a good example is the *grete booke* of Sir John Paston.)[2] Similarly the ephemeral nature of the commonplace book excludes those MSS. whose contents were planned in advance, such as Robert Thornton's book of romances, BM Addit. 31042,[3] or the large 'aureate' collections and finely produced books such as BM Addit. 37787,[4] which has well-executed illuminated initials. On the other hand it is not necessary to exclude books compiled by different hands, as long as it is sufficiently evidenced that the book was regarded as a depository for miscellaneous items (an example of a book compiled by different hands is Harley 3810, pt. I, an *Orfeo* MS.): in any definition of a commonplace book the emphasis should be on the word 'miscellaneous'.

Every commonplace book has its own history: **T** began life as an account book for the abbey; Sloane 747 (early xvi c.) is primarily a register of Missenden Abbey, but enough oddments were added to it for Robbins to class it as a commonplace book.[5] Some books began as scrapbooks for miscellanea, but eventually became specialized: Harley 941, for instance (xvi c., described as 'J. Edwardi Collectanea'), begins with a great mixture of items but gradually becomes specialized in mathematical and astronomical material; Egerton 1995 opens (ff. 3ᵃ–45ᵇ) with a text of the *Seven Sages of Rome*, continues with a large section of miscellaneous items (including a list of 'Proper Terms', the

---

[1] See Robbins, *SL*, pp. 237–8.
[2] See H. S. Bennett, op. cit., and C. F. Bühler, 'Sir John Paston's *Grete Booke*, a fifteenth-century "best-seller"', *MLN* lvi (1941), 345–51.
[3] See Greene, *SEC*, p. 174, and bibliography given there.
[4] Ed. N. S. Baugh, *A Worcestershire Miscellany* (Philadelphia, 1956).
[5] Robbins, *SL*, Introduction, p. xxx.

Book of Courtesy, etc.), but devotes most of its later parts to a London Chronicle.[1]

Some of the best examples of the genuine commonplace book are: Balliol 354 (xvi c.), compiled from both manuscript and printed sources by the London grocer Richard Hill and others;[2] Tanner 407 (late xv c.), owned by Robert Reynys of Acle, Norfolk; Harley 3362 (xvi c.), a very scrappy but fascinating collection of short items, often proverbs and weather-lore, mainly in Latin; Lansdowne 762 (late xv c.), a neatly written collection of short texts, many in English; Sloane 1584 (see above); Harley 3810, pt. I (see above); Harley 2252, ff. 1ᵃ–53ᵇ and 133ᵃ to the end (these sections are sixteenth-century, and form the commonplace book of John Colyn of London);[3] the Brome MS.;[4] Porkington 10;[5] parts of Bodley Lat. misc. c. 66;[6] Trinity College, Cambridge, O.2.53, a small paper book (late xv c.) with very neatly written contents in both English and Latin.[7]

(ii) *Contents of Trinity College, Cambridge, O.9.38*

T can rival any of these books in the catholicity of its contents, which are drawn from the literature of three centuries. It includes English and Latin, prose and verse, clerical and

[1] C. L. Kingsford, *English Historical Literature in the Fifteenth Century* (1913), p. 96; K. Brunner, *The Seven Sages of Rome*, EETS, 191 (1933), pp. xi–xii.

[2] Ed. R. Dyboski, *Songs, Carols and Other Miscellaneous Poems from the Balliol MS. 354*, EETS, ES 101 (1907); full description by Sir R. A. B. Mynors, *Catalogue of the MSS. of Balliol College, Oxford* (1963), pp. 352–4. Some parts of the MS. (a transcript of which is in Balliol College Library) were also edited by Flügel: see Bibliography. For the relationship between Balliol 354 and T, see above p. 23, n. 3.

[3] See R. H. Robbins, 'Consilium domini in eternum manet (Harley 2252)', *Studia Neophilologica*, xxvi (1953–4), 58–64.

[4] Ed. Lucy Toulmin Smith, *A Commonplace Book of the Fifteenth Century* (1886). The manuscript is now in Yale University Library.

[5] See A. Kurvinen, 'MS. Porkington 10', *Neuphilologische Mitteilungen*, liv (1953), 33–67. The MS. (which was compiled by several different hands) belongs to Lord Harlech, but is deposited in the National Library of Wales.

[6] See the typescript Bodleian 'Summary catalogue of medieval MSS. acquired 1916–1964', and R. H. Robbins, 'The poems of Humfrey Newton, Esq., 1466–1536', *PMLA* lxv (1950), 249–81.

[7] James, *Catalogue*, iii. 169–74, gives a full account of the MS.

popular, satirical and devout, practical and entertaining, medieval and humanistic. Several items, printed in Appendix I, owe their inclusion to their local Glastonbury interest: they are Nos. (I), X, XIX–XX, XXVI, XLIX, and L. It is also possible that Nos. XXVIII and XLVIII were of interest to **T** because they mention the abbey, the former in a passage contrasting the merits of Glastonbury with the behaviour of one of its monks, and the latter relating the translation of St. Hilda's relics from Whitby to Glastonbury. Some other items could also be said to have local interest: No. XIII, 'De Symonia et Avaritia', is almost certainly by a canon of the neighbouring Wimborne Minster in Dorset (Walter of Wimborne, who wrote in the thirteenth century); as remarked above, No. 16 is a verse which was also written on the refectory wall at the Austin Priory of Launceston, Cornwall; Nos. LVI and LVII are a hymn and prayer in honour of St. Uritha, patron saint of Chittlehampton, Devon.

Of the English prose, Nos. 1 and 2 are medical recipes, 3 is a copy of a letter sent from Paris giving probably an eyewitness account of the pageant which greeted Henry VI before his coronation there in 1431; 14 is a curious piece about absurd folly (perhaps originally in verse and concluding a sermon exemplum); 19 is a list of fifteen qualities to be sought in a horse. The English verse includes a long poem in couplets on gardening (No. 4, 'The Feat of Gardeninge'), perhaps an abridgement and translation of a Latin treatise; a collection of proverbs in couplets (23); two anti-feminist poems (5 and 12, of which 12 is probably by Lydgate); four poems of religious moralizing (6, 8, 9, 22); a Marian lament (21); three secular moral poems (7, 10, 18). Of the shorter English poems, 13 is a stanza playing on the various senses of the word 'good', 15 follows No. XXIV, 'Death', and is a macaronic mortality poem, 16 concerns good manners when visiting, and 17 is a short verse advising against giving away one's goods (the conclusion of a well-known sermon exemplum). Nos. 1–12, the bulk of the English contents, were entered in the MS. at the same time.

The Latin may conveniently be divided into prose, major and

minor, and verse, major and minor. The accounts (1) were written some time before the scribe began to use the book for literary entries. There are three full-length stories: No. xiv recounts the miracle of the boy of Toledo, who was murdered by the Jews but continued to sing the *Alma Redemptoris Mater* (in this form it is one of the closest analogues to the Prioress's Tale); No. xvii is another version of the 'Wager on the Wife's Fidelity', not previously known; No. xliv is a translation, made in 1436 or 1438, by Leonardo Bruni of Arezzo of Boccaccio's story of Tancred of Salerne, Guiscardo, and Ghismonda. No. l is a copy of a letter from Nicholas Frome, Abbot of Glastonbury, relating news (sent to him at Cologne) of the events in Bohemia during the Hussite wars. Nos. lii–liv are the well-known pieces of religious apocrypha concerning the History of the True Cross, and the legendary lives of Pilate and Judas Iscariot. Of the shorter prose pieces, xi describes *luxuria* under the image of the Chimera and its tripartite body. xxxii is a note attributed (erroneously) to Bede, denouncing the evil of priests who fail to celebrate the Mass. xlvii is a note taken from John the Deacon's *Vita S. Gregorii*, and concerns the efficacy of prayer on behalf of those detained in hell. xlix concerns permissible rations in the abbey (taken from former Abbot Henry de Blois). lv is an allegory describing the cloister and its buildings in terms of virtues.

A large number of the long poems are satirical: ii is the extremely popular 'Apocalypsis Goliæ', an attack on clerical corruption; iv is a similar attack 'De virtute clavium', on the vices of monastic officers; also anti-clerical but more light-hearted is viii, the burlesque description in deliberately bad Latin of a monastic feast and quarrel; v, 'De quatuor raptoribus', and xxii, 'Tempus acceptabile', are serious complaints on the evils of the age. More humorous satires are iii, 'De poena coniugii', a well-known anti-feminist diatribe, and xxxiii, 'Descriptio Northfolchiæ', an account of the follies and imbecility of the people of Norfolk. xxvi, 'Ingratitudo', by Stephen Deverell of Glastonbury, is a serious attack on the vice of ingratitude.

Although the first 200 lines of XIII, 'De Symonia et Avaritia', are, as the late title says, a complaint on the vice of avarice and the power of money, the theme changes to that of mortality and the omnipresence of Death (for an account of its author, Walter of Wimborne, see below, pp. 62–3); also on Death is the dramatic XXIV. There are two debates, VII, 'Water and Wine', and XXI, 'Summer and Winter'. VI is a dream-vision allegery which interprets the worship of Christ in musical terms. There are several simple religious poems: X, 'Epitaph on Joseph of Arimathea', XIX–XX, 'Hymn and prayer to the two St. Josephs (of Nazareth and Arimathea)', XVIII, 'Epiphany hymn', XLV, 'Nativity hymn', LVI–LVII, 'Hymn and prayer to St. Uritha'. XLVIII, over 600 lines of Leonine hexameters, is a semi-historical, semi-devotional life of St. Hilda of Whitby, with a section on Cædmon and a final account of the Norman refoundation of the abbey. There are several poems of historical interest: XXVIII–XXXI are closely linked, and concern the fourteenth-century friars: XXVIII is by Richard Tryvytlam, a Minorite, who laments the treatment of the friars in Oxford; XXXI, 'De supersticione Phariseorum', is a reply to Tryvytlam by an anonymous monk; XXIX complains of the attacks on the friars by Richard Fitzralph and (probably) his associate Richard Kilwyngton; XXX, 'De astantibus crucifixo', is a short but pleasant story at the expense of the friars, and provides a bridge between the friars' complaints and the reply. Also historical are XLI and XLII, two very skilful parodies of hymns by Venantius Fortunatus: they celebrate the death of the hated favourite Piers Gaveston. IX, 'The Stores of the Cities', is a humorous piece on the characteristics of seven English cities; it is written in 'dog-Latin' (following No. VIII, which is deliberately ungrammatical).

Most of the short verse pieces are proverbial, 'medical', or religious: simple proverbs are XII, XXVII a–b, XXXV (with an English translation), XLIII a–c; semi-proverbial are XXIII (the things which bring contentment), XXXVI (Peter Comestor's epitaph, a mortality lyric), XXXIX, 'Fortune', and XLVI, 'The vanity of earthly things'. A simple medical piece is XXXIV, 'De quatuor complexionibus'; often classed with medical material are drinking songs, of which we have three examples, xv, xxv, and xliiib. The following are religious: xxxviii, 'The Eucharist', xl, 'The *Agnus Dei*' (this verse accompanied the gift of an artificial lamb), and li, a copy of a religious pardon. xxxvii consists of two lines 'interpreting' the name vvillelmvs: it was perhaps composed in honour of an abbey patron.

(iii) *Principles of selection*

The fifteenth century was a turning-point in the history of English literature: the beginnings of the 'humanistic' movement may dimly be discerned, and poets, perhaps for the first time (in the vernacular), began to be conscious of 'literature', of poetic excellence which had nothing to do with *sentence* or even with *myrthe*. Terms of art began to creep into their vocabulary, concerned with elegance, ornateness, and polish: it was in the immediately post-Chaucerian decades that there arose the new poetic technique of 'aureation', a purely poetic use of Latinate vocabulary for decorative purposes. Poets began consciously to view their work as (to use the language of Northrop Frye) 'centripetal', self-sufficient organisms. In such an age of change it is important for modern historians of literature to know something about the tastes of the reading public, to be aware not only of what was written but also of what was read. The possibility that poets were writing in a way other than that expected by their readers is also of consequence to the sociologist: the separatist notion of 'culture' as distinct from profit or entertainment is perhaps one of the most important determining factors in the developments of modern literary taste. Manuscripts are often regarded simply as the vehicles for the transmission of literary texts from one age to another, but they may also be considered as documents of literary importance in their own right: an anthology may be simply a useful collection of texts, or it may be an index of the tastes of the individual who compiled it, and through him even of the tastes of a generation. It is, then, of no small significance to observe what an educated reader in the thriving community of Glastonbury, fully aware of and well able to select from a great variety of texts, actually thought worthy of inclusion in his anthology.

What kind of a man was it that compiled this miscellany? What were the tastes and interests that defined and limited his selection? His high degree of literacy has already been indicated by his linguistic proficiency. He was also a scribe of moderate competence: he makes mistakes, to be sure, but most of them are the result of haste rather than failure to understand what he was writing (his handling of the 'humanistic' Latin of No. XLIV is a singular exception). The extent of his reading and interests is amply shown by the variety of the entries, and by the wide net which he cast in his search for material. He was led to include several items associated with his own abbey, but he did not do so merely out of *pietas*: the 'Glastonbury items' themselves cover a variety of interests, and, with the exception of No. I (made before the MS. was adapted to literary purposes) and perhaps No. XLIX, there is no place in the MS. for abbey material of purely parochial interest.

He evidently had a great liking for satire: the first four entries in the book are all satires, and satire and complaint dominate the whole collection. Much of it is serious complaint, but, like so much medieval satire, its aims are general rather than particular, hitting not at specific persons or groups but at vice in general. Perhaps No. IV, 'De virtute clavium', is the only one which deals with a specific, identifiable, group of people—the monastic office-holders. In this respect the compiler merely reflects the taste of his age—or rather, of the preceding age, for the high period of this kind of writing was the thirteenth century: most of the 'Goliardic' collections, associated frequently with names such as Golias, Gauterus, etc., date from then. The targets of such satires were usually vague, the Church administration or women and so on; the Martial-like bite of a Serlo de Wilton was rare. This type of unspecific moral denunciation had great popularity among English vernacular writers (particularly Lydgate) of the fifteenth century, and the scribe's selection mirrors the fashion of his generation: the bitter invective of Skelton was yet to be written. The manuscript also contains a good deal of not very serious satire, of which the anti-feminist poems (Nos. III, 5, and 12) are a good example: in the Middle Ages there were essentially three streams of anti-feminism—the religious (Jerome), the philosophical (Theophrastus, and Walter Mapes's *Epistola Valerii ad Ruffinum*), and the popular. It is to this last class, which emphasizes the practical inconveniences of marriage for the ordinary man, that the three pieces in this MS. belong; in this too the compiler reflects the tastes of his age. The only serious moral piece on the subject (No. XI) significantly is directed not against women but against the vice of *luxuria*.

The compiler's fondness for humorous items is fully exemplified by XXXIII, 'Descriptio Northfolchiæ'; the humour of this poem is not subtle; it is the naïve schoolboy delight in stories of stupidity and folly, typified by the tales of Owlglass and the Men of Gotham. Closely akin to this kind of humour is burlesque, and two poems (VIII and IX) derive their humour simply from the fact that they are written in deliberately bad Latin—another schoolboy joke. On the other hand, this joke is illuminating: there is a kind of sophistication in the ability to play with the normally rigid rules of grammar, to distort English so that it looks like Latin, in order to demonstrate one's dexterity. A further extension of the desire to 'play' with language is parody, and two poems in the MS. (XLI–XLII) are parodies of famous hymns—they are, admittedly, serious in that they celebrate the death of the hated Piers Gaveston, but the same element of delight in linguistic dexterity is present. It is perhaps in this element of 'dexterity', rather than in the broad humour of the Norfolk poem, that we begin to get an idea of the scribe's personal tastes: one of the general characteristics of his entries is their 'neatness', their use of single (or at most two or three) metaphors around which they build their whole structure. The 'meaning' of a poem is never hard to find: it is stated as expressly as possible with the aid of one or two simple devices of imagery or rhetoric. I shall mention below the absence of aureation in the English poems; in the Latin prose and verse there is rhetoric in plenty, but the rhetoric is obvious (so obvious as to be objectionable in No. XVII), and is simply superficial ornament. Narratives progress from beginning to end, and the rhetoric rests on the surface. Related to this liking for the intellectually conceived (but not very complex) scheme, is the absence of strongly emotional poems such as dramatic appeals to sentimentality for religious purposes; an exception is the address of the Virgin (No. 21), but even this poem makes part of its appeal by the traditional juggling of the paradox of the son–father–brother relationship of Christ to man. Pathos is confined to the prose stories: the lost boy of Toledo and his desperate mother (XIV), the grief of the falsely accused wife (XVII), and the tragic love of Guiscardo and Ghismonda (XLIV). But we find none of the violent assaults on the emotions made by mystics like Rolle or by the Franciscans with their affective use of *le pathétique*.

Most of the English poems are refrain-lyrics (employing the eight-line stanza such as the ballade); the moral (religious or worldly) lesson of the poem is repeated as the final line of each stanza: the fullest collection of such poems, very popular in the late fourteenth and fifteenth centuries, is in the Vernon MS. The compiler's liking for such poems is important for negative reasons: although he knew Lydgate's works (Nos. 11 and 12), he chose to select from them the more traditional type of poem, rejecting the aureate diction and rhetorical elaboration then in favour among poets. In this sense it might be true to describe the selection as 'non-literary' in that it neglects the current fashions in poetry. The absence of any 'courtly' lyrics is the result not of monkish asceticism (as is clear from the large amount of secular and humorous entries), but perhaps of a native distaste for 'Frenchified' manners and literary habits.

If the fifteenth century is regarded as the period standing between the end of the Middle Ages and the beginning of the Renaissance, the collection is distinctly 'medieval' in its preferences. It is not suggested that in this respect the MS. is at all unusual: indeed, it is part of my argument that in the fifteenth century the 'divisive' aspect of culture had begun to appear, and had started to exclude from an interest in poetry even the educated and literate reader. Many commonplace books of the period show the same tendencies to look backwards to earlier kinds of literature. Many of the Latin items in the MS. were composed in the twelfth and thirteenth centuries, and others for which we have no firm dates resemble earlier products in style and subject: we know that the apocryphal stories (LII–LIV) and many of the satires (e.g. II, III, IV, V, and VIII) were composed in the twelfth or early thirteenth centuries; the two debate poems (VII and XXI) are of the sort common in the same period; whatever the date of 'Gregory's Garden' (VI), its model was the dream-vision allegory such as that of the early 'Metamorphosis Goliæ'. An exception to the preference for earlier material is No. XLIV, the translation into Latin of Boccaccio's story of Guiscardo and Ghismonda by Leonardo Bruni (1436 or 1438); of course, although we may call Bruni himself a humanist and remark on the complexity of his Latin, the story was Boccaccio's; however, we must still admire the compiler for his inclusion of the translation so soon after its publication, and must acknowledge the fact that he has admitted into his MS. a story of conflict and social frustration, of egalitarian sympathies and tragic love.

This search for the compiler's tastes and preferences has perhaps over-stressed an imaginary unity of conception behind the book. It must be remembered that many items were included simply because they were of interest in a variety of ways: the historical pieces, the letters, the gardening poem, and so on, simply demonstrate a collector's curiosity and interest in some of the more unusual literary products in circulation. He shares with many other commonplace books a fondness for proverbs: the fifteenth century was a great age for collections of proverbs (e.g. Rylands Library Latin MS. 394, Douce 52, BM Addit. 37049), and this interest seemed to affect everyone who had a collector's spirit. Balliol 354 and Harley 3362 are good examples of commonplace books that show a particular liking for English and Latin proverbs; neither these books nor **T** organize their proverbs systematically in the way that the collections do; nor, on the other hand, do they use them merely as space-fillers—**T** often makes a group of proverbs the main entry on a page, and No. 23 is a full-length poem consisting entirely of independent proverbs.

Although we have said that commonplace books are almost by definition not planned in advance, nevertheless we must allow **T** the 'intention' of making the collection as varied as possible. It often seems that he would be content to copy several pages of one kind of material, and would then tire of the theme and deliberately change the type of entry. For instance, his first four entries are satirical, but are followed immediately by a religious dream-allegory. Nos. XXVIII–XXXI are all concerned with the friars; they are followed by the light-hearted buffoon-ery of the Norfolk poem—his weariness of the theme of the friars may be indicated by his use of the old formulaic colophon *Explicit expliceat, ludere scriptor eat* at the end of XXIX. His interests were those of a collector, an antiquarian almost like Thomas Hearne himself, who rejected the changing fashions around him, and preferred to amuse himself unpretentiously in the literature and curiosities of the past.

METRE

(i) *English verse*[1]

Of the thirteen full-length English poems nine are refrain-lyrics, with eight- or twelve-line stanzas whose final line is the refrain. Five of the poems with eight-line stanzas, Nos. 5, 9, 11, 12, and 18, have the ballade-stanza, *ababbcbc*: **T**'s fondness for this particular rhyme-scheme is indicated by the fact that he has converted the original rhyme royal (*ababbcc*) of Lydgate's 'Beware the blynde' (No. 12) into the ballade by the addition of an extra *b*-rhyme after the sixth line. Lydgate's 'Ram's Horn'

---

[1] Thesis, i. lxxxii–lxxxiii.

(No. 11) is a *tour de force* in which the same *a*, *b*, and *c* rhymes are kept throughout the poem. The twelve-line stanza of No. 7, *ababababbcbc*, is to be classed with the ballade: it keeps a stanza based on three rhymes only, and repeats the *b*-rhyme before the introduction of the *c*-lines (a feature derived from rhyme royal). Nos. 6 and 10 rhyme *ababcdcd*, No. 8 *ababcdcdefef*.[1]

Of the other long poems, No. 4 is in couplets (the usual metre for ME practical verse), as are the proverbs of No. 23. No. 22 is in four-line stanzas *aaaa*. No. 21 has a complex structure (see below, p. 87). The rhyme schemes of the short poems vary.

(ii) *Latin verse*[2]

The basic line for all poems with quantitative metre is the hexameter; only one poem (No. xxx) and two proverbs have non-rhyming hexameters. The remainder may be classified according to their use of rhyme:[3] the strong break at the caesura made internal rhyme possible in the hexameter. The types are as follows: (*a*) the Leonine hexameter with simple internal rhyme (e.g. xlviii, 1–551), the most common form; (*b*) single-sound Leonine couplets, in which the same rhyme is used internally and finally in two lines (e.g. xlviii, 552–609); (*c*) collateral Leonines, which rhyme in couplets finally and internally . . . *a* . . . *b*, . . . *a* . . . *b* (e.g. xxviib); (*d*) tailed Leonines, which rhyme in couplets, finally only. Many of the short poems (e.g. No. x) consist of a mixture of several types of Leonine. In

---

[1] The ballade-stanza was the most popular metre for religious and secular moralizing in the fourteenth and fifteenth centuries; the following are all in this metre: Brown, *RL XIV*, Nos. 95–120 (except 98 and 114) and 132 (of which 17 have eight-line stanzas, 8 twelve-line stanzas); *RL XV* has 27 eight-line and 4 twelve-line ballades, and Robbins, *SL*, 14 eight-line ballades (mainly love poems). Other examples of the stanza scheme *ababcdcd* include *RL XV*, Nos. 52, 107, 144.

[2] Thesis, i. lxxxiii–xc. The metres employed in the Latin verse are all quite common, and receive full treatment by Meyer and Norberg; however, many of the metrical variations (particularly those in the asclepiadic line) have not been analysed before, and treatment of the rhythmical asclepiad has hitherto been sketchy and somewhat inconsistent.

[3] See Meyer, i. 82–5, Norberg, pp. 64–9.

all the quantitative verse in the MS. there are many departures from Classical Latin vowel quantities; for some of these departures there are sound reasons which accord with the practice of Medieval Latin versification in general (e.g. automatic lengthening of a short vowel at the caesura); others may show normal Medieval Latin quantities, or may be the result of poor versification. There are hardly any cases of elision; hiatus is quite common.

Of the rhythmical metres the most popular is the rhythmical asclepiad, 6 pp+6 pp,[1] used in nine major poems (Nos. II–IV, VI, XIII, XXIV, XXVI, XXVIII, and XXXIII). This line derives from the accentual prose reading of the Classical quantitative asclepiad: the result is a twelve-syllable line broken into two halves of six syllables. Because of Classical practice, each half may be read as either (a) xxxxxx or (b) xxxxxx; if two (a) types are put together, the final syllable of each half develops secondary stress, and the total line can be read as an Alexandrine xxxxxxxxxxxx; if two (b) types are put together, the result is a dactylic tetrameter. Variations[2] on this line include: first half-line with five syllables; first half-line with paroxytonic stress (both these variations are very common); first and second half-lines with an extra unstressed syllable (this variation is rare: in some cases the lines may be corrupt). The normal stanza for the rhythmical asclepiad is four lines aaaa, except for No. XXXIII, which has stanzas of uneven length. Rhymes are normally disyllabic, but few poems achieve consistency throughout.

Six poems have the popular Goliardic line, 7pp+6p, the

---

[1] Norberg's descriptive signs (p = final paroxytonic stress, pp = final proparoxytonic stress) are adopted in this analysis. For earlier descriptions of the rhythmical asclepiad, see Meyer (whose analyses are very inconsistent), i. 30, 226–8, 297–302; iii. 19, 38, and Norberg, p. 99.

[2] None of these variations is noted by Meyer or Norberg. The line in which the first half has five syllables only, x x x x x x / x x x x x x, may also be read as a rhythmical alcaic, which is discussed as a separate verse-form by Meyer, i. 225–6, Norberg, p. 101. The phenomenon of paroxytonic stress in the first half-line, producing 6p+6 pp, is implicitly denied by Meyer, iii. 199, who observes 'deshalb schließen die Kurzzeilen aller Alexandriner mit Proparoxyton'. However, lines beginning with this rhythm are very common in the poems in T (e.g. XIII. 13, *Jesus omnibonus*, 131, *veri simulacro*).

favourite metre for satire and invective. Variations, recorded by Meyer,[1] include: extra unstressed syllable in the first or second half-lines, and a first half-line with the unusual rhythm x́xxx́xx (instead of x́xx́xx́x); a variation *not* noted by Meyer is the second half-line with the rhythm xx́xx́x (instead of x́xx́xx), but this is almost entirely confined to one poem (XXIX) and may be an idiosyncrasy. All poems with the Goliardic line have four-line stanzas *aaaa* except XXXI, which is in couplets; XXIX has internal rhyme through each stanza (though some of the rhymes fail) and a couplet 'O-and-I' refrain (see below p. 77). Final rhymes in Goliardic stanzas are always disyllabic.

These are four poems in the metre of the regular Victorine sequence, 2, 3, or 4 (8p), 1(7pp), *aa(aa)b cc(cc)b*; one of them is the burlesque poem No. VIII. The last three stanzas of XVIII show a progressive increase in size, from *aabccb* to *aaaabccccb*: this feature is found in other Victorine sequences of the twelfth century (see below p. 119). In XIX and LVI there are some lines which have too many syllables: these may be explained in various ways (such as the semi-consonantal pronunciation of *i* after a vowel and before a consonant), but some of them may simply be the result of incompetence. Rhymes in the regular sequences (except in VIII) are usually disyllabic.

No. XLV is in rhythmical iambic dimeters. On the parodies of hymns by Venantius Fortunatus in which quantitative lines are adapted to rhythm and rhyme, see below pp. 87–8. There is no certain case of elision in any of the rhythmical poems, and many examples of hiatus.

---

[1] Meyer (i. 250–6) states that these variations are found only between the eleventh and thirteenth centuries, that he has found them only in Goliardics, and that they are attributable to the influence of vernacular poetry: he had found them only in poems written in Germany. His principal discussions are: extra unstressed syllables in first and second half-lines, i. 251; change in rhythm, i. 307–11.

DESCRIPTIVE INDEX

ROMAN numerals refer to Latin entries, Arabic to English. Each entry, apart from the English recipes and those items printed in Appendix I, is presented as follows: folio ref., title (which may be that of **T**, or one of the later hands (**D** or **A**), or may be editorial), opening and closing lines, colophon (if one is given in the MS.); reference to Walther, Chevalier, *Index*, etc.; list of other MSS.; list of principal editions (including my own thesis) and discussions; account of any textual relationships; synopsis or brief discussion of the entry; metre.

In texts and lines quoted from the MS. all abbreviations (which are standard and require no comment) are expanded without indication. Words or letters in square brackets [. . .] are restorations (where the MS. is damaged or deficient); words and letters in angled brackets ⟨. . .⟩ are editorial emendations.

For all bibliographical abbreviations, see the Bibliographical Index at the end of the book. Other abbreviations are as follows:

BM	British Museum
BN	Bibliothèque Nationale
CL	Classical Latin
CUL	Cambridge University Library
ME	Middle English
ML	Medieval Latin
OE	Old English
OF	Old French
T	Trinity College, Cambridge, MS. O.9.38 (main hand)
T.C.C.	Trinity College, Cambridge
WS	West Saxon

The present location of the following MSS. is not repeated: in the British Museum, MSS. Cotton, Egerton, Harley, Lansdowne, Royal, and Sloane; in the Bodleian Library, Oxford, MSS. Ashmole, Digby, Douce, Rawlinson, and Tanner; in the National Library of Scotland, MSS. of the Advocates' Library collection.

I

ACCOUNTS

See Appendix I, p. 102. This damaged list of figures probably represents the assessment for papal dues made on the Abbey and its extensive holdings. From the colour of the ink it is evident that this entry was made some time before the one on the following page.

1

f. 1ᵇ ENGLISH MEDICAL RECIPE (damaged)

Thesis, i.1. This seven-line recipe was added at the same time as No. 2 on f. 16ᵇ: see above, p. 5. The title is obscured by damp; the ingredients and instructions are so common that there is no way of telling what the recipe was intended to cure. Other edited collections of recipes include: Gottfried Müller, *Die Prosarezepte des Stockholmer Miszellankodex X. 90* (Kölner anglistische Arbeiten x, 1929); G. Henslow, *Medical Works of the Fourteenth Century* (1899); M. S. Ogden, *Liber de Diversis Medicinis*, EETS, 207 (1938).

II

f. 2ᵃ APOCALYPSIS GOLIÆ

f. 2ᵃ A Tauro torrida lampade Sinthii
Fundente iacula feruentis radii

.   .   .   .   .

f. 7ᵃ Nisi papaueris cena sophistica
Mentis vestigia fecisset lubrica
Explicit Apocalipsis

Walther 91. Ed. K. Strecker, *Die Apokalypse des Golias* (Rome, 1928); Wright, *Mapes*, pp. 1–20, and frequently: see Raby, *SLP* ii. 214–19. Strecker lists over sixty MSS.: T shares the extra stanza of Group β (see Strecker, p. 39), and has the normal English version of st. 17.

The poem was among the most popular of the Middle Ages: in a vision the poet first meets Pythagoras, on whose body are seen all the arts and sciences; Pythagoras leads him to all the famous scholars and poets of antiquity; an angel appears and reveals to the poet a vision which he is to write to the seven churches of England, as John had written his Revelation to the seven churches of Asia; most of the vision is taken up with the book with seven seals, fair outside but foul within; each seal reveals the evil life of bishops, archdeacons, etc. Finally the poet is taken up to the third heaven, but is forced to drink forgetfulness about what he sees there and only allowed to relate what his guide inscribes on his head.

Metre: rhythmical asclepiads; 111 four-line stanzas.

III

f. 7ᵃ DE POENA CONIUGII (*De coniuge non ducenda*)

f. 7ᵃ Sit Deo gloria laus benediccio
      Johanni pariter, Petro, Lauren[cio]

   .   .   .   .   .

f. 9ᵃ Non est in tartara quies aut ocium
      Nec dolor coniugis habet remedium.
         Qui capit vxorem litem capit atque dolorem
            Explicit Magister Walterus Mape de Pena
            Coniugii.

Walther 18302; Chevalier 33539. Ed. Wright, *Mapes*, pp. 77–85, etc. See Lehmann, *Parodie*, pp. 117–19; Raby, *SLP* ii. 222–3. Walther notes that over sixty MSS. are known (with several different *incipits*): **T** is most similar to the text of Cotton Vespasian E. xii, which ends at the same point as **T**, thus omitting the final three stanzas which make a proper conclusion; both MSS. and Cotton Titus A. xx omit (Wright's numbering) 101–4, but of MSS. known to me **T** alone places 153–64 after 76, where they are most inappropriate.

   This satirical attack on marriage was immensely popular; it is quoted in the Wager Story (XVII below, pp. 66–7). It emphasizes neither the virtues of virginity (as Jerome had done) nor the obstacles in marriage to the life of a philosopher (as Theophrastus and Walter

Map), but simply the discomforts for an ordinary working man; the mores are those of the public house rather than the cloister, though there is no shortage of learned references. The poet relates that he was on the brink of marriage when God sent three angels 'in the valley of Mamre' to dissuade him; they were Peter of Corbeil, John Chrysostom (who also has characteristics of the Evangelist, being compared to an eagle), and one Lawrence: the assumption that this was Lawrence of Durham was based on the erroneous attribution of the poem to the latter in a Paris MS. Each spoke in turn and stressed the rigours of a household with a nagging wife (frequent reference is made to the Book of Proverbs), and the infidelity and insatiability of women. The poet accepted their arguments.

Metre: rhythmical asclepiads; **T** has 48 four-line stanzas.

The proverb before the colophon is written by hand **B**.

IV

f. 9ª   DE VIRTUTE CLAVIUM

f. 9ª   Noctis crepusculo brumali tempore
        Pausans [in lect]ulo mens ausa temere

                    .   .   .   .   .

f. 10ª   O vos qui legitis michi ignoscite
         Quod vobis displicet illud corrigite.
             Explicit materia de virtute clauiu⟨m⟩.

Walther 11891; Leyser, pp. 785–6. Also in: Cotton Vespasian A. xviii (late xiii c.), f. 168ᵇ (**V**); Cotton Titus A. xx (xiii c.), f. 163ᵇ (**Ti**); Rawlinson B. 214 (xv c.), f. 167ª (**R**); Corpus Christi, Cambridge, 481 (xiii c.), p. 453 (**C**); Harley 3362 (xvi c.), f. 28ᵇ, fragment only (**H**); College of Arms, Arundel xxx (late xiii c.), f. 7ᵇ; Bodley James 7 (after 1628), pp. 55–7 (**J**).

Ed. thesis, i. 2–7, ii. 197–202, from all MSS. except Arundel; Wright, *Mapes*, pp. 187–90, from **Ti**, **V**, and **H**, with several errors.

J is an acknowledged copy from the Arundel MS., but may have been contaminated by **T**, which James examined (see above, p. 7). On the basis of common errors, discussed fully in my thesis, the relation between MSS. can be shown diagrammatically (see p. 43): it is very unlikely that any MS. other than **J** was copied directly from any of the others.

The poem is a simple and commonplace attack on abuses of power by monastic office-holders and the consequent corruption in the life of the cloister. The poet relates that he could not sleep, but continually thought of the degeneration of monastic life, of the flattery, the backbiting, the bribery, and the duplicity now prevalent; the officials regard their power, not as a privilege and duty, but as an instrument to suppress criticism; the humble get no advancement; he ends with a plea for forgiveness if he has spoken too rashly. The poem concentrates its message through three puns: the *claves*, 'keys', symbols of the office-holders in the *claustrum*; *adulacio*, 'flattery', properly originating *ab aulicis*, which has now found a home in the monasteries; finally and most thoroughly, *obedientia* 'the monastic discipline', which has now been perverted by the obedientiaries, the office-holders, to mean not their own obedience but the obedience due to

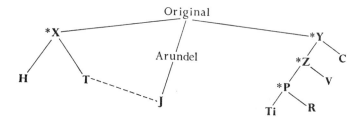

them from other members of the community. There are one or two possible references to the 'De Palpone et Assentatore' (Wright, *Mapes*, pp. 106–30); the image of those who seek favour by going around plucking imaginary feathers from the coats of their superiors is found in 'De Palpone', 271–4, 285–6, but also in Alanus ab Insulis's *Planctus Naturae* (*PL* ccx. 431–82), col. 469: the origin of the idea may be in Ovid's *Ars amatoria*, i. 149–52. On the whole reference is made not to the Vulgate but, with bitter irony, to the *Benedictine Rule*. The author may have been an outsider, a friar or member of the secular clergy, or a member of a community who had been frustrated in his hopes of office.

Metre: rhythmical asclepiads with many variations; **T** has 27 four-line stanzas.

V

f. 10ᵇ   DE QUATUOR RAPTORIBUS

f. 10ᵇ   Licet mundi vicia cunctis exorare
Nam in mundo video multos nunc errare

. . . . .

f. 11ᵃ   Et dum sumus validi penitere gratis
Vt possimus alibi gaudere cum beatis. Amen.
Hec materia precedens est de quatuor raptoribus.

Walther 10311 and 11427. Also in: Harley 978 (xiii c.), f. 123ᵇ (H);
Bodley 828 (late xiv c.), f. 46ᵃ (B).

Ed. thesis, i. 7–10, ii. 203–5; Wright, *Pol. Songs*, pp. 46–51 with
a translation. See Raby, *SLP* ii. 210; Manitius, iii. 932. Walther
incorrectly ascribes the *incipit* of H to T, and vice versa. The three
texts vary little: after 60 H has an extra stanza; B and T both have
individual errors, but it is theoretically possible that H is the direct
antecedent of either MS.

The poem is a bitter denunciation of the evils of the times; the
world continually deteriorates; no one can get advancement without
force, money, or litigation; evil has spread through the whole community, both religious and secular; impiety rules and charity grows
cold. The evils can be attributed to four brothers: Robert (i.e.
robber), Richard (rich and hard), Gilbert (*gylur*, 'deceiver'), and
above all Geoffrey (*yeo fray*, 'I will do it—later', the symbol of pro-
crastination). The poet ends with a prayer to be allowed to repent
for his own sins. H (xiii c.) gives a *terminus a quo* for the composition,
which is partly confirmed by the Anglo-Norman form *yeo fray*; the
pronounced final -*e* of *ryche* 58 gives no further indication of date.
Raby places the poem 'in the school of Walter of Chatillon' but will
not allow that it is by Walter himself because of various irregularities
in the metre. Wright regards the four brothers as historical, but they
are almost certainly to be taken as types of social evil. The interpretation of Geoffrey and Richard is also found in Rylands Library,
Latin MS. 394 (*Rylands Proverbs*, p. 112), and Raby compares the
etymologizing in Walter of Chatillon's 'Quis furor, o cives': *Moral-
ische-satirische Gedichte*, ed. K. Strecker (Heidelberg, 1929), No. 15,
p. 133.

Metre: Goliardic with many variations; T has 21 four-line stanzas.

VI

f. 11^b GREGORY'S GARDEN (*De Musica et Organis*)

f. 11^b Peccator nimium polluti labii
       Possessor lucidi rarus ingenii

. . . . .

f. 12^b Nunc regem seculi sonet vox hominum
       Et omnis spiritus collaudet dominum. Amen.
       Explicit materia precedens.

Walther 13905. Ed. A. G. Rigg, 'Gregory's Garden: a Latin dream-allegory', *MÆ* xxxv (1966), 29–37; thesis, i. 10–14, ii. 205–12. Otherwise unnoticed.

The poem combines all the most noted features of the medieval dream-allegory; in his dream the poet passes through *devia* and comes on Gregory's garden, outside which flowers abound, birds sing, and a stream waters the meadow. The poet lies down by the stream, but an eagle comes down and tells him to leave the blandishments of the water and to follow him. The poet explains that the *devia* represent the miseries of the world, the garden is the church, the song of birds the praise offered to Christ, and the eagle God himself. He follows the eagle into the garden, where he sees the *doctores musice*—Tubal, Pythagoras, Boethius, Gregory, Guido, and Franco. Finally he sees Orpheus playing the organ, which the eagle interprets allegorically: the sounding-boards (or shutters) represent the fragile human substance, the keys are the senses, the bellows are the vital spirit of man, the pipes are the praises of the faithful, and Orpheus himself is the presiding rational spirit. The vision ends, and the eagle returns to heaven. Let everyone sing in praise of God.

The possible debt to the 'Metamorphosis Goliæ' (Wright, *Mapes*, pp. 21–30), the use of an eagle as guide and mentor (as in Chaucer's *House of Fame*, combining the functions of both Dante's eagles), and above all the constant references to music and musical history, are all discussed in my edition. The poem was written certainly after 1280 (the approximate date of composition of Franco of Cologne's *Ars cantus mensurabilis*), and perhaps even after the *House of Fame*.

Metre: rhythmical asclepiads; 27 four-line stanzas.

VII

f. 12ᵇ   DEBATE BETWEEN WATER AND WINE

f. 12ᵇ   Dum tenerent omnia medium tumultum
Post diuersas epulas et post vinum multum

·   ·   ·   ·   ·

f. 13ᵇ   Et laudaui continens patrem natum flamen
Terminans in gloria dei patris. Amen.
Explicit.

Walther 4975 (cf. 3834, 5270, 6220). Ed. Wright, *Mapes*, pp. 87–92,
and frequently. See Walther, *Streitgedicht*, pp. 46–9; Raby, *SLP*
ii. 284–5.

As Walther lists some MSS. twice it is impossible to be certain
about the number of texts; there are certainly more than twenty,
English and foreign. It is impossible on the evidence available to me
to establish T's relationship with other texts: it often differs from
Wright's text and frequently fails to make sense. After 98 (Wright's
numbering) T omits forty-eight lines without loss of sense, and after
150 omits four lines.

The poet says that after a drunken banquet he dreamed that he
was snatched up into the third heaven, where he witnessed a debate
before God between Thetis (Water) and Lyaeus (Wine); the arguments concern the pleasure and profit each brings to man, and mainly
depend on Biblical parallels. The debate concludes with the victory
of Wine.

Metre: Goliardic; T has 29 four-line stanzas.

VIII

f. 14ᵃ   SATYRICUM IN ABBATES

f. 14ᵃ   Quondam fuit factus festus
Et venerunt ad commestus

·   ·   ·   ·   ·

f. 16ᵃ   Et riserunt pre gaudiatus
Et totus mutauit in bordia. Amen.
Explicit.

Walther 16347. Ed. W. Meyer, 'Ein Gedicht in Spottlatein', *Nachrichten von der königlichen Gesellschaft der Wissenschaften zu Göttingen. Philologisch-historische Klasse* (1908), 406–29; frequently printed, usually on the basis of Meyer's edition: e.g. S. Gaselee, *Oxford Book of Medieval Latin Verse* (1928, repr. 1946), No. 95, pp. 173–5 (extracts only). See Raby, *SLP* ii. 307–8.

There are many MSS., both English and foreign, and in a poem like this (written in deliberately bad Latin) readings naturally differ considerably. It is impossible to construct even a plausible stemma. The longest versions are two English ones, T and Harley 913 (early xiv c., H).

The poem is a burlesque: an abbot and prior sit down to drink; the abbot asks that the other brothers join them, but the prior says this would be improper; a canon stands up and attacks the prior, and the two indulge in a long flyting; finally they reach agreement and sit down to drink (probably leaving the poet still without a drink). The Latin is deliberately ungrammatical: rules of gender, number, tense, mood, etc., are regularly broken; words are given unusual terminations and vernacular words are twisted into Latin. Meyer (p. 408) regards the poem as an English composition: in T the abbot and prior belong to *Leycestris*, in H to *Glowcestrus*; other texts have *cocletestus, clocestum, cum claustralis*, the last two against the rhyme. The English words in T quoted by Meyer might equally be French (but perhaps add *totum cum silvestria*, 221, ? 'all in silver') and in any case argue only for T. To this evidence Meyer adds what he calls the 'English humour' and the reference to beer.

Metre: regular Victorine sequence, 3 (8p), 1 (7pp) *aaab*; many lines do not have the correct number of syllables; the *b*-rhyme is on *-ia* throughout. In T there are 62 stanzas.

IX

f. 16ᵇ THE STORES OF THE CITIES

f. 16ᵇ Hec sunt londonis pira pomusque regia thronus
Chepp stupha cok lana dolium leo verbaque vana

. . . . .

Et princeps tumba bel brachia sulsaque plumba
Et syserem potus—hec sunt staura ciuitotis.

Walther 7596. Ed. A. G. Rigg, *Anglia*, lxxxv (1967), 127–37; thesis, i. 15–16, ii. 214–22; *Rel. Ant.* ii. 178 (this edition has no notes or explanations, but several errors).

The poem is written in a mixture of dog-Latin and English. There are seven three-line stanzas, each of which lists the 'properties' of an English city, not particularly seriously, e.g. 'these are London's: pear and apple [sceptre and orb], palace, throne, Cheapside, the Stews, Cock Lane, the "Tunne", the "Lion" [? an inn] and empty words, lance and shields—these are the stores of the city.' The cities (listed in the left-hand margin of the page) are London, York, Lincoln, Norwich, Coventry, Bristol, and Canterbury. The Tun (2) ceased to be a prison in 1401, and it is possible that in 14 reference is being made to the new steeple of St. Michael's Church in Coventry, erected in 1373. There appears to be no connection with other poems on the properties of cities or counties (e.g. Neckham's *De laudibus divinae sapientiae*, v. 691 ff., ed. T. Wright, RS xxxiv (1863), pp. 456 ff., or 'The propyrte of euery shyre', *Index* 3449, *Rel. Ant.* i. 269 and ii. 41).

Metre: approximate Leonine hexameters; all stanzas have the 'refrain' *hec sunt staura ciuitutis* (*-etis, -atis, -otis*) except the fourth and fifth.

2

f. 16ᵇ   FOR THE FLUXE

Thesis i. 16. This is a twelve-line prose medical recipe in English; for collections of recipes, see on No. 1 above, which was entered in the MS. at the same time as this.

3

f. 17ᵃ   THE PARIS PAGEANT FOR HENRY VI
(December 1431)

> f. 17ᵃ   And as towchyng tydynggys of thys contre the kyng
> came vnto Parys from Seynt Denys the secunde day
> of December and ther was he

.   .   .   .   .

f. 18ᵃ   an ther schall be vnto the day afore hys Coronacyon
that schall be on Sonday the viij dayes afore Cryste-
messe day.

This prose account is also found in the 1445 Continuation of the
London Chronicle, which is found in: Trinity College, Cambridge,
O.9.1 (xv c.) f. 208ᵃ (B); Cambridge University Library, Hh. 6. 9
(xv c.) f. 177ᵇ (U); Harley 540 (xvi c.) f. 40ᵇ (H). Printed from B,
with footnotes (not always complete) from U, by F. W. D. Brie, *The
Brut*, EETS, 136 (1908), 458–61. See C. L. Kingsford, *English
Historical Literature in the Fifteenth Century* (1913), pp. 91–4.
Thesis, i. 16–20, ii. 223–34. See my article in *N. & Q.* ccxi
(1966), 324–30.

U is an incomplete version of the Chronicle (and a leaf is missing
just before the end of this passage); H is a copy made by Stow, but
was not made from the version represented by BU. The existence of
T has not previously been noticed: it is evident from the use of
schall in the last line that the original from which T was copied was
written soon after the events that it describes, unlike the other texts,
which refer to the coronation in the past (except U which inconsistently uses both preterite and future). From the style of the opening
it seems likely that T is a copy of a letter.

The correspondent tells of the arrival of the young King from
Saint Denis due north of Paris and his progress down the Rue St.
Denis; he met various civic officials on his entry; the route was filled
with pageants, mimes, symbolic tableaux, etc. A real ship modelled
the arms of the city; model hearts opened to release doves, to show
that Paris opened its heart to him. The King crossed on to the Île
de France; the English texts report that he visited Notre-Dame, but
this is denied by the French versions. The procession continued east-
wards, passing St. Paul's; the King spent the night with the Duke
of Bedford, and the following morning visited the Queen of France
before leaving for Bois-de-Vincennes to await his coronation. The
route can best be appreciated from the *Atlas des anciens plans de
Paris en facsimile* (*Histoire générale de Paris*, Paris, 1880).

Detailed accounts of the pageant are also found in the following
French texts, all of which are independent of each other: Letter-
book K in the Guildhall, ed. J. Delpit, *Collection générale des documents français qui se trouvent en Angleterre* (Paris, 1847), pp. clx–clxi
and 239–44; R. R. Sharpe, *Calendar of Letter-books . . . of the City of
London* (1899–1912), Letter-book K, pp. 135–7; the *Journal d'un
bourgeois de Paris*, ed. A. Tuetey (Paris, 1881), pp. 274–6; the

Chronique d'Enguerran de Monstrelet, ed. L. Douet-d'Arcq, 6 vols., *Soc. de l'hist. de France* (Paris, 1857–62), v. 1–6. It has hitherto been assumed that the English account was based on that in Letter-book K; in my article referred to above I give reasons for disputing this assumption, and for believing that the English account was written by an eyewitness of the procession.

4

f. 18ᵇ   THE FEAT OF GARDENINGE

See below, Appendix I, pp. 103–16.

5

f. 21ᵃ   PLUK OF HER BELLYS AND LET
                HERE FLEE

f. 21ᵃ   Who carpys of byrddys of grete jentrys
         The sperhawke me semyth makys moste dysporte

         .   .   .   .   .

f. 22ᵃ   Then speke ye here feyre and loke ye plesant be
         And then pluk of here bellys and let here fly.
                                Explicit.

Index and *Suppl.* 4090; *Crooked Rib*, No. 365. Ed. thesis, i. 27–31, ii. 249–52. Also found in Rawlinson C. 86 (xvi c.), f. 59ᵇ (**R**). Printed from **T** in *Rel. Ant.* i. 27–9; from **R** by R. Cords, 'Fünf me. Gedichte aus den Hss. Rawlinson poetry 36 und Rawlinson C. 86', *Archiv*, cxxxv (1916), 292–302. Both these editions have some misreadings.

T has thirteen stanzas, **R** eight only in the following order: I–III, VII, V, IX, VI, and a final stanza which is an amalgamation of X and XI. The **R** version is quite self-contained, but a slight confusion in the pronouns of its final stanza suggests that at that point at least it is making a deliberate abridgement.

The poem is an anti-feminist satire; it uses extensively an image from hawking: the poet relates that he tamed a sparrow-hawk, best of all birds, and equipped it in the most expensive way with lunes and jesses, but in time it turned out to be 'ramage' and searched for another mate; the poet allowed her to do so, taking off her bells and letting her fly away. This is what one should do with one's mistress, however beautiful she may be: all women are fickle, they will reduce one's finances, but always they will be lecherous and prone to adultery; this does not refer to good wives but to young women who will deceive their husbands.

For the theme in anti-feminist satire, see *Crooked Rib*, pp. 47–8. For this refrain, see *Crooked Rib*, No. 108, and for similar ones cf. Lydgate, *Troy Book*, iii, 4342, ed. H. Bergen, EETS, ES 103 (1908), 520; *Rel. Ant.* i. 75–7; Robbins, *SL*, No. 181 and No. 41/4. No poem develops the image as thoroughly as this one. A long and elaborate warning against fickle mistresses is illustrated in terms of fishing and fowling in 'A man that lovyth fyscheng', *Crooked Rib*, No. 7, *Index* 71.

Metre: ballade-stanza, *ababbcbc*.

6

f. 22ª   REVERTERE

    f. 22ª   Yn a noone hete of somerday
           The sone schone full mery that tyde

        .   .   .   .   .

    f. 23ª   And ofte to fall yn wykkyd sorte
           Then ys the beste Reuertere.
           Explicit Materia Ista

Index 1454. Also found in: Lambeth Palace 853 (early xv c.), p. 61 (L); Balliol 354 (xvi c.), f. 155ᵇ (B). Ed. thesis, i. 31–4, ii. 252–5; printed from L by Furnivall, *Hymns*, pp. 91–4; from B by Flügel, 'Liedersammlungen', pp. 168–9; Dyboski, p. 80; *EEL*, pp. 195–6.

T has eleven stanzas, to which L adds four after st. XI; B has only four stanzas, I–III and XI; neither T nor L, both of which have individual errors, can be the source of either of the other MSS.

The poem is a typical moral *chanson d'aventure* (see Sandison *passim* and p. 39, n. 76). The poet goes hawking with his dogs; they raise a pheasant but as the poet runs after it he is caught by a briar whose leaves are inscribed with the message *Revertere*; he is reminded of the sins of his youth, his pursuit of pleasure and his self-centredness (youth is symbolized by the hawk, pleasure by the pheasant). All man can do is to turn back (*revertere*) from his sins.

For the refrain cf. Greene, *EEC*, No. 140 (*SEC*, No. 37), *EEC*, No. 269; *Carm. Bur.* I, 2, No. 181. The first and last may be referred to Cant. 6: 12, but the second, like the present poem, whose theme concerns God's infinite mercy, is probably derived from Isa. 44: 22 'revertere ad me quoniam redemi te'.

Metre: eight-line stanza, *ababcdcd*.

7

f. 23ᵃ   WHO SAYTH THE TRUTH SHALL
BE SHENTE

f. 23ᵃ   Who so wyll leue yn ese
And hys worschypp woll not alayne

.   .   .   .   .

f. 23ᵇ   Thys lesson lerne ye of me
Who seyth sothe he schall be schent.
Explicit

Index 3420. Also found in: Bodley Vernon (1380–1400), f. 408ᵇ, col. 2 (**V**); BM Addit. 22283 (Simeon MS. 1380–1400), f. 130ᵃ, col. 3 (**S**). Ed. thesis, i. 35–7, ii. 255–9. Printed from **V** by Varnhagen, pp. 301–4; Furnivall, *Vernon MP*, pp. 683–6; Brown, *RL XIV*, No. 103: the readings of **S** were collated by Varnhagen and Brown.

As is well known, **S** and **V** are closely related, often sharing *minutiae* of spelling (cf. also No. 9 below). **V** cannot be copied from **S** (cf. *RL XIV*, No. 95, 76–9, note on p. 276), but it is possible that **S** is an intelligently corrected copy of **V** with some additional poems not in **V**). In the present poem **SV** have two additional stanzas after st. II, and reverse sts. III and IV. **T** is unusually corrupt and often fails to make sense (omitting two lines after 10). The 'editorial' practice of **SV** makes it likely that the order and number of stanzas in **T** represent the original.

The poem is a bitter denunciation of the times, when no one dares to tell the truth. A man must learn to conceal the truth and to flatter; it is not safe to talk to anyone in this false world; if a friar dares to preach to the people he is in danger of losing his liberty or his life; even children are faithless, and no one can trust anyone else.

Poems concerned with truth-telling either advise against it in a satirical, worldly fashion, as here (cf. the poems recommending caution—see Nos. 10 and 18, below), or advocate it as a virtuous practice (cf. Brown, *RL XIV*, No. 120, from the Simeon MS., which may have been modelled on the present poem). For the refrain, cf. Lydgate, 'The cok hath lowe shoon', *MP* ii, No. 70/135; *Douce Proverbs*, No. 148, p. 57; *ME Disticha* 122; *Rylands Proverbs*, p. 109. *Metre*: twelve-line ballade, *ababababbcbc*; **T**, which has six stanzas, is deficient in stanza 1.

8

f. 24ᵃ   PARCE MICHI DOMINE

> f. 24ᵃ   By a foreste syde walkyng as y went
> Dysporte to take yn a mornyng
>
> .   .   .   .   .
>
> f. 25ᵃ   God grawnte vs all to se thy blessyd face
> That seyth Parce michi domine.
>   Explicit etc.

Index and *Suppl.* 561. Also found in: Royal 18 A. x (first half, xv c.), f. 119ᵇ (**R**); Stonyhurst XXIII (early xv c.), f. 60ᵇ (**S**); Bodley 596 (early xv c.), f. 21ᵇ (**B**); T.C.C. R. 3. 21 (second half, xv c.), f. 34ᵃ (**T2**); Douce 322 (late xv c.), f. 15ᵃ, col. 2 (**D**); Harley 1706 (late xv c.), f. 16ᵃ (**H**); Bodley lat. misc. e 85 (xvi c.), f. 79ᵃ (**B2**).

Ed. thesis, i. 38–43, ii. 259–65, from all MSS. except **B2**. Printed from **B** by Brown, *RL XIV*, No. 121, and from **D** by Kail, *26 PP*, pp. 143–9.

T is considerably shorter than all other versions (104 lines, against the normal 240); its abridgement may generally have been intentional, but the omission of 121–32 (Brown's numbering) was certainly a mistake, as this stanza introduces the subject of the Third Feather. The thesis edition did not take account of the readings of **B2**, which often agree with **T** against all other MSS. (which may be shown by one common error to derive from the same original); **B2**, however, which breaks off after (Brown's) 122, has two of the stanzas omitted by **T**, and probably confirms the authenticity of the long version: this suggests that the short version of **T** is an editorial abridgement. The stemma posited here is based on a great number of common errors (deficient rhymes, repetitions, omissions of lines, and essential words, etc.) and is discussed for all MSS. except **B2** fully in my thesis.

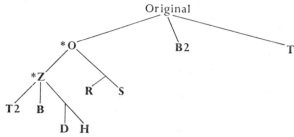

For the close relationship of **D** and **H**, see Brown, *RL XIV*, p. 286, and A. I. Doyle, 'Books connected with the Vere family and Barking Abbey', *Essex Archaeological Soc. Trans.* N.S. xxv (1958), 222–43. Either both shared a common original, or **H** was copied from **D**.

The poem is another *chanson d'aventure*: the poet is walking in a forest, and comes across a glade where birds are singing; one of them has no feathers and cannot fly; it tells the poet that it once had four feathers, Youth, Beauty, Wealth, and Strength; each had led it into many sins, but one by one they had fallen away; only God's mercy can now help. The poet thanks the bird, and recognizes the value of the prayer *Parce michi, Domine*. The device of a talking bird to give moral counsel of this sort is not uncommon: cf. *The Quatrefoil of Love*, ed. I. Gollancz and M. M. Weale, EETS, 195 (1934), and Sandison, p. 39, n. 74. The refrain (based on Job 7 : 16) is also that of the poem known as 'Pety Job' which precedes this poem in **D** and **H** (printed from **D** by Kail, *26 PP*, pp. 120–43).

Metre: in **T** the poem consists of twelve-line stanzas, *ababcdcdefef*, except for stanza 11, which is eight-line, *ababcdcd*. The long version also has stanzas of sixteen and twenty lines.

9

f. 25ᵇ   AND EVER MORE THANKE GOD
OF ALL

f. 25ᵇ   By a wey wandryng as y wente
Soore y sorowed forsownyng sadde

. . . . .

f. 26ᵃ No better comforte y can se
But euere thanke God of all.
Explicit

Index 562. Also found in: Bodley Vernon (1380–1400), f. 409ᵃ,
col. 1 (**V**); BM Addit. 22283 (Simeon MS., 1380–1400), f. 130ᵇ, col.
2 (**S**); Cotton Caligula A. ii (first half, xv c.), f. 68ᵇ (**C**); Princeton,
Garrett 143 (first half, xv c.), f. 47ᵃ (**G**); Ashmole 343 (early xv c.),
f. 169ᵃ (**A**); Sloane 2593 (*c.* 1450), f. 19ᵇ (**S1**).

Ed. thesis, i. 43–7, ii. 265–71. Printed from **V** by Varnhagen,
pp. 306–9 (with readings from **S**), and Furnivall, *Vernon MP*,
pp. 688–92; from **C** by Halliwell, pp. 225–8; from **G** by R. K. Root,
'Poems from the Garrett MS.', *Englische Studien*, xli (1910), 360–79
(text on pp. 374–6); from **S1** by T. Wright, *Songs and Carols from
a Manuscript in the British Museum* (Warton Club, 1856), pp. 56–9,
and by B. Fehr, 'Die Lieder der Hs. Sloane 2593', *Archiv*, cix (1902),
33–70 (text on pp. 59–62); from **A** by Brown, *RL XIV*, No. 105
(with a discussion of all other texts, p. 279).

The distribution of stanzas in each text is as follows:

T	SV	C	G	S1	A
1	1	1	1	1	1
2	2	2	2	2	2
3–6	3–6	3–6	3–6	3–6	3–6
	*A–*E				
7	7	7	7	7	7
8	8	8	8		8
9	9	9	9	9	9
10	10	10	10	10	
		*F	*F		
11	11	11		11	11
12	12			12	
	2				

It should be observed that Brown is wrong in saying that **SV**
retain Cotton's 'stanza 11' (= *F above), and accordingly his
account of the development of the poem is undemonstrable. It
seems more likely that **T**'s version is closest to the original, that **S1**
and **A** independently made omissions, that **SV** altered the position
of stanza 2 to the end of the poem, and inserted five new stanzas
(for their 'editorial' habits, cf. on No. 7 above), and that the ancestor
of **CG** inserted the new stanza *F—see thesis, loc. cit., for the
close relationship of **C** and **G**.

The poem is a typical refrain-ballade of the Vernon-type: the poet is wandering along the road when he is led by the lane to some writing on a wall (this is clearly the correct reading of line 5); this instructs him to thank God for everything: whatever fortune befalls one, it is God's will, which always gives us better than we deserve; Job was a good example of this. The moral of the poem translates the line from the Mass *Deo gracias* (1 Cor. 15: 57), which in addition to its frequent use in carols (cf. Robbins, *HP*, No. 32) was also used in two refrain poems which frequently have verbal echoes of this one: *RL XIV*, Nos. 96 and 99. The argument of the poem is frequently obscure, and often illogical: this may in part explain the textual corruption of all versions.

Metre: ballade-stanza, *ababbcbc*.

10

f. 26ᵇ   HYRE AND SEE AND SAY NOT ALL

f. 26ᵇ   Throwe a towne as y com ryde
　　　　　Y saw wretyn on a wall

.　　.　　.　　.　　.

f. 27ª   Therefor y rede thynke on thys thyng:
　　　　　Hyre and se and sey not all.
　　　　　　　　　Explicit

Index 3715; found only in **T**. Ed. thesis, i. 48–50, ii. 272–3; Sandison, pp. 121–3. This is not a holograph copy: **T** is in error at 47–8, and the rhyme *seyth*: *peese* 38–40 shows that this is not the original dialect of the poem. There is a four-line introduction followed by 8 eight-line stanzas.

The poet is riding through a town and sees written on a wall the lesson 'Hear and see and say not all': quiet courtesy is the best policy; it does not pay to complain about all that is evil; by reticence men have advanced to high positions, but tale-telling can bring bad results. The moral is worldly, but not satirical like the advice to silence in No. 7; similar poems are: No. 18 below, Lydgate's 'See myche, say lytell and lerne to soffar in tyme', and 'The Cok hath lowe shoon' (*MP* ii, Nos. 67 and 70, pp. 800–1, 813–18), 'Ewyre say wylle or hold the styll' in *Early English Miscellanies*, ed. J. O.

Halliwell (Warton Club, 1855), pp. 62–5, and 'Lerne say wele, say litel or say no3t' in Kail, *26 PP*, pp. 14–22.

For the refrain, cf. 18. 46

> Hyre and see and hold the stylle

and 'Yong Children's Book' (*Babees Book*, pp. 17–25), p. 23/101:

> Here and se and sey thou nought

See also *ODEP* 'Hear and see' and 'Hear much'. Somewhat similar are poems advising patience, e.g. 'For the better abyde' (*RL XV*, No. 183).

Metre: eight-line *ababcdcd* (st. 1 four lines only).

11

f. 27ᵃ   AS RY3TH AS A RAMS HORNE

f. 27ᵃ   All ry3tfowsnes now doth procede
      Syttyth crowned lyke an emperas

.   .   .   .   .

f. 27ᵇ   Thys eche astate ys gouyrned yn sothnes
      Conveyd by lyne ry3t as a rammys horne.

Explicit

Index and *Suppl.* 199. Also found in: Bodley 686 (first quarter, xv c.), f. 190ᵇ (**B**); Huntington Library, EL 26 A. 13 (*olim* Ellesmere; probably before 1456 according to information kindly supplied by Prof. H. C. Schultz), f. 18ᵃ (**E**); Harley 4011 (second half, xv c.), f. 1ᵃ (**H1**); BM Addit. 29729 (xvi c., a Stow MS.), f. 10ᵃ (**Bm**); Harley 172 (xv c.), f. 71ᵇ (**H2**); Ashmole 61 (late xv c.), f. 5ᵇ (**A**); Lansdowne 409 (xv c.), f. 265ᵇ (**L**); Advocates' Library, 1.1.6 (Bannatyne MS., 1568), f. 79ᵇ (**Ba**); Harley 2251 (second half, xv c.), f. 20ᵃ (**H3**); BM Addit. 12195 (? mid xv c.), f. 121ᵇ (st. 6 only, much altered). The old *Index* reference to Pepys 2553 (the Maitland Folio MS.) p. 187 is incorrect: it was taken from Brown *Register*, i. 526.

Ed. thesis, i. 50–3, ii. 273–8. Printed from **H2** by Halliwell, pp. 171–3; from **Ba** by Ritchie, *Bannatyne MS*, ii. 201–2; from **E** by MacCracken, Lydgate *MP*, ii. 461–4, with readings from all texts except **A** and BM Addit. 12195. There are also other minor editions: see *Suppl.*

The distribution of stanzas in each text is as follows:

T, B, E, H1, Bm, H2	A	L	Ba	H3	(BM Addit. 12195)
1	1	1	1		
2	2	2	2		
3	3	3	3		
4	5	4	4		
5	4	6		5	
6	6	5	6	6	6
	*A				
	*B				
	*C				
7	7	7	7	7	
		*D			

For detailed comments on the relationship of the MSS., see thesis, ii. 274: **Bm**, a Stow autograph, was almost certainly copied from **H2** —the colophon to this poem in **Bm** reads 'writen out of mstr. philyppes boke', and **H2** contains a great number of marginal notes in Stow's hand. **B**, **E**, and **H1**, may belong to the same textual family, but this, like other possible relationships, is difficult to establish: the obvious popularity of the poem makes contamination between MSS. quite likely. The single stanza of BM Addit. 12195, although considerably altered, bears some resemblance to that of **A**.

The poem is a satirical denunciation of the times; each stanza lists all the ways in which society is prospering because of the reformed morals and altruistic behaviour of the people, and then denies what has preceded by the refrain 'just as a ram's horn (is straight)!' MacCracken (*MP* i, Introduction, p. xxv) accepts the ascription to Lydgate by **B** and **H2** (followed by **Bm**); there is every reason for agreeing with this on literary grounds: Lydgate was very fond of the satirical *balade per antifrasim*, in which each stanza asserts its own falsehood. Each stanza of 'Vndir your hood is but oo contenaunce' (*MP* ii. 432–3) ends

> As I goo loos and teied am withe a lyne.

Lydgate *RS* 6169–6202 is an exaggerated encomium on women, against which are written the marginal notes *per antifrasim* and *per contrarium*. Lydgate also translated the French poem 'Le mounde va en amendaunt' with the refrain,

> So as the crabbe gothe forward.

(Both French and English versions in *MP* ii. 464–7): on the rhyme scheme of the 'Crab', see below. Other examples of this sort of satire include 'Religious pepille leuyn in holynesse' (Robbins, *HP*, No. 63), refrain,

> Stablenesse foundon, and spesialli in atire,

and the well-known poem from Balliol 354 (Robbins, *SL*, No. 38; Dyboski, pp. 112–13) which has the refrain,

> Of all creatures women be best,
> Cuius contrarium verum est.

Cf. also the anti-mendicant 'Orders of Cain' (Robbins, *HP*, No. 65).

The origins of this sort of satire are in France; one of the earliest instances is the *Évangile aux Femmes*, ed. G. C. Keidel (Baltimore, 1895) whose stanzas usually end with an impossibility, e.g. A-text, 55–6:

> Si seür fait entr' eles mener et joie et feste,
> Que s'on estoit on mer sans mast on grant tempeste;

there are similar poems by Deschamps; see further *Crooked Rib*, pp. 165, 263–4. Robbins, *HP*, pp. 330–1, J. Huizinga, *The Waning of the Middle Ages* (1924; Penguin, 1955), pp. 306–7.

Metre: ballade-stanza, *ababbcbc*. The *a*-, *b*-, and *c*-lines rhyme throughout the poem, a *tour de force* also found in Lydgate's 'So as the crabbe' and its French original (see above), and 'Horns Away' (*MP* ii. 662–5); in the Introduction to 'Say the best' (*MP* ii. 795–6) the *b*- and *c*-lines rhyme throughout, and probably also the *a*-lines if line 1 is an error.

12

f. 28ᵃ   BEWARE THE BLYND ETYTH
MENY FLYE

f. 28ᵃ   Lokyth well abowte ye that louers be:
Let noȝt yowre lustys lede yow to dotage;

> .   .   .   .

f. 28ᵇ   Lett passe ouer yn ese and let the wynd blow:
Beware, the blynde ettyth many a flye.
Explicit

Index and *Suppl.* 1944. Also found in: T.C.C. R. 3. 19 (late xv/early xvi c.), f. 207ᵃ (**T2**); Harley 2251 (mid xv c., a Shirley MS.),

f. 154^b (**H**); Venerabile Collegio Inglese, Rome, Z. 27 (second half, xv c.), f. 75^b (**R**); Stow's *Chaucer* (1561), sig. P3 (last page). The old *Index* reference to Tanner 407 (followed by *Crooked Rib*, p. 180) is incorrect, as noted by Robbins (see below) and *Suppl.*

Ed. thesis, i. 54–6, ii. 278–82. Printed from **T2** by Skeat, *Chaucer*, vii. 295–6, and Robbins *SL*, No. 211; from Stow by A. Chalmers, *English Poets*, 21 vols. (1810), i.¹564; from all except **R** by R. T. Davies, *Medieval English Lyrics* (1963), pp. 238–40. For **R** see R. H. Robbins, 'A Middle English diatribe against Philip of Burgundy', *Neophilologus*, xxxix (1955), 131–46: **R** was not known to Robbins at the time of his edition in *SL*.

T differs from other texts in the addition of a final (seventh) stanza. Other texts have the rhyme royal stanza, *ababbcc*, to which **T** has added a penultimate *b*-line, converting the stanza to the ballade. All other texts reverse stanzas v and vi, so that v is their final stanza. Stow's edition was almost certainly based on **T2**, with which it shares many minor textual details; they both reverse stanzas iii and iv. Otherwise no textual relationships can be postulated. The additions by **T** are almost certainly 'editorial'.

The poem is a standard piece of anti-feminism, emphasizing the instability and treachery of women; the only striking feature is the frequent use of proverbs. Other short anti-feminist poems by Lydgate include 'Beware of Doubleness' and 'Examples against Women' (*MP* ii. 438–45). This poem is discussed in full in *Crooked Rib* (No. 166), pp. 180–1.

The arguments for Lydgate's authorship of this poem (denied hesitantly by MacCracken) are presented in full in my article 'Some notes on T.C.C. O.9.38', *N. & Q.* ccxi (1966), 324–30. Essentially, they depend on the fact that the Earl of Suffolk was probably alluding to this poem when he attacked Lydgate for his anti-feminism: for Suffolk's poem, 'How the louer ys sett to serue the floure', see H. N. MacCracken, 'An English friend of Charles of Orleans', *PMLA* xxvi (1911), 142–80 (text on pp. 168–71). The proverbial refrain of this poem is common: see Skeat's note, and *Crooked Rib*, No. 239; it is the last line of the stanza on the 'Trials of Old Men in love' (Robbins *SL*, No. 176).

Metre: ballade-stanza, *ababbcbc*, in **T** only: see above.

X

f. 28^b   EPITAPHIUM D. JOSEPH

Not in Walther, and previously unprinted and unnoticed. See below, Appendix I, p. 117. The poem is a literary 'epitaph' on Joseph of Arimathea who, according to medieval tradition, was buried at Glastonbury.

Metre: six lines of 'mixed' Leonine hexameters.

XI

f. 28^b   NOTA DE LUXURIA

Notandum quod luxuriam precedunt ardor et petulancia; concomitantur fetor et inmundicia; secuntur dolor et tristicia siue penitencia, vnde luxuriosi Chimere comparantur, vnde versus:

> Ex triplici forma constat monstrosa Chimera
> Parte leo prima, media caper, anguis in yma;
> Hanc formam retinent Venerem quicunque frequentant:
> Vt leo non trepidi pergunt implere quod optant,
> Fetent vt capri petulantes luxuriosi,
> Ritu serpentis pungunt nouissima scorti.

The verse is not recorded in this form by Walther, and I have not met with the prose elsewhere; thesis, ii. 283–4. See Walther 4473, 13370, 16455; Hauréau *NE* iv. 282; W. Wattenbach, *NA* xviii (1893), 520.

   The earliest use of this image known to me is by Marbod of Rennes, *Liber decem capitulorum*, ed. W. Bulst (Heidelberg, 1947), iii, 'De Meretrice', 45–9. The ultimate source was Lucretius, *De rerum natura*, v. 905 (cf. Isidore I, xl. 4). A later use is found in Walter Mapes's *Epistola Valerii ad Ruffinum*, which circulated on its own but was also included in the *De nugis curialium*, ed. M. R. James (*Anecdota Oxoniensia*, 1914), Dist. iv, Ch. iii; the Chimera passage is on p. 144 of James's edition—it was used by Lydgate *RS* 3370–8, and quoted in the margin of the MS.

Metre: mixed Leonine hexameters.

XII

f. 28ᵇ   Dicentes E vel A   quotquot nascuntur ab Eua

Not in Walther or *Sprichw*. The line is from Peter Comestor's
Historia Scholastica (*PL* cxcviii, 1071). The metre requires *dicunt*.

XIII

f. 29ᵃ   DE SYMONIA ET AVARICIA

f. 29ᵃ   Relatu plurium interdum audio
          Infausti Symonis infausto cambio

.   .   .   .   .

f. 36ᵇ   Oremus Dominum in sopibilibus
          Vt nos sidereis coniungat cetibus.
          Finis Tractatus de Morte

Walther 16560 (*incipit* misread); the title and colophon are by **A.**
There is no other MS. Ed. thesis, i. 57–85, ii. 284–96. It has not
been noticed elsewhere.

The poem is in two parts: the first (1–220) is about the power of
Money (*Nummus*); the second (229–836) tells of the invincibility of
Death. Although 229 begins with a rubric initial, and hand **A** heads
the page (f. 31ᵃ) *Mors inexorabilis*, there is no reason to believe that
there were originally two separate poems: 221–8 prepare explicitly
for the change of theme, and the two halves are stylistically very
similar. The first half emphasizes the rebirth of Judas's crime, which
has spread over the world: Truth cannot compete with Money at
court or anywhere; the two root evils in the world are Avarice and
Flattery, but the former is the concern of the present poem: let Truth
yield. Money cannot, however, conquer Death: Death ignores
riches, beauty, intelligence, and courage; Death is equal to all, and
makes all equal. Its messengers are seen in every living thing on
earth, but few people take any notice. Let us purify our hearts, so
that we may be joined with God. (The diffuse and repetitious style
makes it impossible to give a detailed synopsis).

The poem is almost certainly by Walter, a member (at this time) of the college of secular canons at Wimborne Minster, Dorset. At 133–4 he writes

> Sed de palponibus hic nichil cudimus
> De quibus alias diffuse scripsimus.

This seems to refer to the poem 'De Palpone et Assentatore', ed. Wright, *Mapes*, pp. 106–30 (Manitius, iii, 271; Raby, *SLP* ii, 223–4) which is 'signed' by Walter (574, 614, etc.); the 'De Symonia' has many verbal echoes of the 'De Palpone', and both poems share a fondness for elaborate rhetorical devices such as *anaphora*. Both poems show great learning, quoting liberally from Terence, Horace, Persius, Isidore, etc., and have a wide vocabulary of exotic words of Greek origin. Equally, they share a rambling style and an extra-ordinarily long-winded method of argument. The case for identity of authorship is set out fully in my thesis.

This Walter is almost certainly identical with the Walter of Wimborne, O.F.M., who was a Franciscan lector at Cambridge 1261–3 (or 1263–6) and who spent the later part of his life at Norwich. He was the author of a prose treatise on the four elements (preserved in CUL MS. Ii. 2.27) and of several (equally longwinded) poems on the Vanity of the World, in honour of the Virgin, etc. See A. B. Emden, *Biographical Register of the University of Cambridge to 1500* (1963), s.v. Wynbourne; Beryl Smalley, *English Friars and Antiquity in the early Fourteenth Century* (Oxford, 1960), pp. 50–1, 365–8; *AH* 1, 630–43; Raby, *CLP*, p. 455. The works of the Norwich Walter (which were known to Leland, Bale, and Pits) have not previously been linked with the 'De Palpone', except in a brief note by A. G. Little (ed.), *Fratris Thomae . . . de Eccleston 'Tractatus de Adventu Fratrum Minorum in Angliam'* (1951), p. 58. I am in the process of preparing an account of Walter of Wimborne and a full edition of his works. Wright conjectured that the *regi tenero* to whom the 'De Palpone' is addressed (615) was Henry III in his minority (1216–23); if this is correct, we must allow Walter a long career as a writer.

Metre: rhythmical asclepiads in four-line stanzas; disyllabic rhyme is achieved more successfully here than in any other poem in the MS. except No. XXIV.

XIV

f. 37ᵃ   DE CANTU 'ALMA REDEMPTORIS
MATER'

f. 37ᵃ   Cum mater gracie sui memorum immemor nequa-
quam existat, iugiter ipsius est memoria memoranda
. . .

.   .   .   .   .

f. 39ᵇ   . . . cum effectu, que sui memores Deo commendet
meritis et iuuet beneficiis. Amen.
Finis

This story, found in this form in **T** only, is printed in full by
W. F. Bryan and G. Dempster, *Sources and Analogues of Chaucer's
Canterbury Tales* (Chicago, 1941, repr. 1958), pp. 480–5. For minor
corrections to their edition, see thesis, ii. 297.

This is No. C 10 of the Bryan and Dempster analogues to the
'Prioress's Tale', and is in fact one of the closest parallels to Chaucer's
version. A young boy of Toledo learns the song *Alma redemptoris
mater* and walks through the Jewish quarter of the town singing it;
his throat is cut by the Jews; when his mother goes out to search
for him, she hears him still singing the song, for the Virgin has placed
a pebble on his tongue; he is disinterred, but continues to sing. By
the prayers of the congregation he is restored to life; when the pebble
is removed he points out his murderer but pleads for mercy for him:
the Jew is converted, baptized, and pardoned.

The title and *Finis* are by hand **A**, which has also added at the foot
of f. 37ᵃ the proverb

Non vox sed votum, non musica cordula sed cor,
Non clamans sed amans sonat in aure Dei.

This is also found in T.C.C. O.1.31 (James, *Catalogue*, iii. 36) and
Rylands Proverbs, p. 109. See Werner *Sprichw.*² N272. p. 83.

XV

f. 39ᵇ   DE POTANDI NUMERO

f. 39ᵇ   In potu primo purgantur guttura limo;
Gaudia sunt nobis solempnia, quando bibo bis;

.   .   .   .   .

Et quia credo mori, potabo de meliori:
Hic bonus est potus—bibatur illico totus!

Walther 9052; there are many MSS., only a few of which I have seen.
Ed. thesis, i. 85–6, ii. 297–8. See also W. Wattenbach, *Anzeiger*, xxvi
(1879), 98. Versions tend to differ slightly from each other.

The poem is a simple twelve-line drinking song 'by numbers': for
similar numerical compositions, see the references given by Walther,
and cf. No. xxv below.

Metre: Leonine hexameters; line 8 is short of a syllable.

13

f. 39ᵇ   A POEM OF GOODS

Ho hath good, can good—a wyse man he ys holde;
Ho hath no good, can no good—a wyse man hyt me tolde;
Hyt ys not good for no good, a man to be to bolde;
Ther ys no good but Goddys good but hyt wull flet and fold.

Index and *Suppl.* 4083. Also found in: University College, Oxford,
MS. 33 (xv c.), f. 68ᵃ (**U**); Advocates' Library 1.1.6 (Bannatyne
MS., 1568), f. 75ᵃ (**B**).

Ed. thesis, i. 86, ii. 298–9; printed from **U** by Brown, *RL XV*,
No. 189, and from **B** by Ritchie, *Bannatyne MS.* ii. 184.

B is a single stanza, like **T**, but has six lines *aaaabb*; **U** is a poem
of four stanzas, each of four lines (eight according to Brown's lay-
out) plus a two-line *V-and-I* refrain (cf. No. xxix below): the first
stanza of **U** corresponds to **T** and **B**. The poem is an elaborate piece
of word-play on the various senses of the word 'good': in **T** the basic
sense is preserved, but much of the word-play is lost (e.g. in line 2
read *gode* for *wyse*: a *godeman* is the head of a household or an inn-
keeper, *OED*, *MED*). The stanza in **B** is very corrupt and the sense

obscure. However, **B** and **U** agree in the presence of a two-line refrain: such a refrain is the mark of a long poem. **T** may be an extract from such a long poem, or **U** may be an expansion of a shorter conceit as represented by **T**.

XVI

f. 39ᵇ X gratus nisi sis, bis pulcher, tri quoque fortis,
     Quater sapiens, quin dis, sex sanctus, amodo non sis.

Not in Walther. The couplet also occurs in Balliol 354, f. 201ᵃ (Dyboski, p. 134), with one or two minor differences. It is clearly a riddle or conundrum of some sort, but its exact nature is obscure; in the Balliol MS. it follows the maxims *Aristotolis ad Alexandrum magnum* and precedes a couplet on dicing: it may be in fact connected with dicing, but it is marked as a distinct item in the Balliol MS.

XVII

f. 40ᵃ THE STORY OF THE WAGER

 f. 40ᵃ Fuerunt olim in Anglia duo milites incliti, animosi, victoriosi in operibus bellicis, generosi, speciosi

    . . . . .

 f. 44ᵃ peruenerunt feliciter ad gaudia repromissa, vbi cum eis semper frui vita sine termino nobis donet invictus leo, leo victor in patibulo. Amen.
       Explicit Fabula

Ed. A. G. Rigg, *Romania* lxxxviii (1967), 404–17; thesis, i. 86–97, ii. 300–9. It has not been noticed before.

  It is a version of the story of the 'wager on the wife's fidelity' which, from one branch, contributed to Shakespeare's *Cymbeline*; another well-known occurrence of it is in Boccaccio's *Decameron*, ii. 9. As related by **T**, the story is this: there were once two famous English knights, one married (*A*), the other a bachelor (*B*); at the instigation of his wife *A* tries to dissuade *B* from his debauched life. *B* replies with an attack on women, and says that *A*'s wife will be unfaithful if given a chance; they wager all their property on the bet. During *A*'s absence, after unsuccessful attempts at seduction, *B* steals a ring from the wife while she is bathing, and uses it to convince *A* that he has succeeded. *A* denounces his wife, and leaves home; the wife goes in search of him; she disguises herself as a man and enters the service of the Emperor, eventually rising to the rank of seneschal. The two knights arrive at the court, but recognize neither the woman nor each other. The woman challenges *B* to single combat, kills him, and is reunited with her husband.

The most thorough analysis of the story-type is by Gaston Paris, 'Le cycle de la gageure', *Romania*, xxxii (1903), 481–551. The **T** version has elements from several of Paris's different classes, but no analogue contains all the elements found in **T**. For a full discussion of its relation to other versions, see my edition in *Romania*, or thesis, ii. 300–3.

The story is told with great rhetorical elaboration, and is decked out with quotations principally from the Vulgate (many of which are grotesquely inappropriate), but also from such standard anti-feminist tracts as the *Epistola Valerii* by Walter Mapes (see above, p. 61), Theophrastus's *Aureolus* (in Jerome's treatise *Adversus Jovinianum*, *PL* xxiii, 277), and the poem 'De coniuge non ducenda' (No. III above, pp. 41–2), and also from Ovid and Boethius. It may have been an exercise in rhetoric: it may even be the work of the scribe of **T**.

XVIII

f. 44ᵃ   EPIPHANY HYMN

See below, Appendix I, pp. 117–20.

XIX–XX

f. 44ᵇ   HYMN AND COLLECT TO THE
              TWO ST. JOSEPHS

See below, Appendix I, pp. 120–2.

XXI

f. 45ᵃ   ESTAS ET HIEMS

> f. 45ᵃ   Quedam nos lassiuia valet confortare
> Quam vobis, si placeat, volo reserare
>
> .   .   .   .   .
>
> Serui tui turgidi semper induuntur;
> Clamant et tripudiant: modo non vtuntur.
> Explicit, etc.

Walther 15059. Unique to this MS., and evidently incomplete. Ed. thesis, i. 101–3, ii. 312–13; Walther, *Streitgedicht*, pp. 209–11. See also my notes in *N. & Q.* ccxi (1966), 324–30; Manitius, iii. 951.

The poem is a conventional debate: Summer and Winter speak alternate stanzas in criticism of each other. There is no conclusion, which probably indicates that the text is deficient; there is, however, no reason to suppose with Walther (op. cit., pp. 44–5) that the victory would have gone to Summer. His arguments, as I have shown in my article, depend on a misreading of the words *et earum contenti*[*o*] which were added to the title by hand **A**. Walther noted a similarity to the debate between Age and Youth, but this is no more than the traditional conflict of gaiety and sadness common to this kind of debate.

Metre: Goliardic, *aaaa aaaa bbbb bbbb*; there are twelve stanzas.

XXII

f. 45ᵇ   COMPLAINT ON THE TIMES

> f. 45ᵇ   Tempus acceptabile, tempus est salutis,
> Tempus est excutere iugum seruitutis
>
> .   .   .   .   .
>
> f. 46ᵃ   In thronos duodecim iudices sedete,
> Super tribus Ysrael regnando quiete. Amen.
> Explicit etc.

Walther 19171, Chevalier 33964; there are various versions beginning with lines later in the text: Walther 465, 9900, 15278, 15780.

Ed. *AH* xxxiii, 289–94 (Nos. 258–9); Wright, *Mapes*, pp. 52–4 (the closest text to **T**, from which the poem has not been printed); see thesis, ii. 313–14, Raby, *SLP* ii. 209–10.

There are at least ten MSS. of the poem, both English and foreign; no clear stemma emerges from those I have examined. The poem is an urgent and vigorous call to repentance, directed in particular at the clergy. The first line is based on 2 Cor. 6: 2.

Metre: Goliardic, in (eighteen) four-line stanzas.

XXIII

f. 46ᵃ   Felix qui poterit: Irato corde tacere
                           Morbo vicioque carere
                           Cum corpore mente valere
                           Justorum gesta docere
                           Mundum virtute replere
                           Viuendo mortua ferre
                           Vitam moriendo tenere

Walther 6348. Found only in **T**.

Metre: hexameters, rhyming finally.

14

f. 46ᵃ   Hoo so maky3t at Crystysmas a dogg lardyner, and
            yn March a sowe gardyner, and yn May a foole of
            every wysmanys counsayll, he schall neuer haue goode
            larder, ne fayre gardyn, nother counsayll well ykeptt.

Index and *Suppl.* 4106. Also found in: Lansdowne 762 (late xv c.), f. 16ᵇ (**L**); Book of St. Albans (1486), sig. F5ᵛ (**A**); Caxton's edition of Petrus de Alliaco's *Meditationes circa septem psalmos poenitentiales*, MS. addition on f. 34ᵇ (**C**).

Ed. thesis, i. 104, ii. 314–15. Printed from **T** in *Babees Book*, p. 358; from **L** in *Rel. Ant.* i. 233; from **C** by C. F. Bühler, 'Middle English Apophthegms in a Caxton volume', *ELN* i (1963), 81–4.

Bühler discusses the relationship of **ALC**: **A** and **L** are probably closely related (see also No. 19, below, p. 74). Similar 'space-filling' items are found in the Plimpton MS., Porkington 10, Balliol 354, and Pepys 1047; the textual relationship between them has not yet fully been analysed.

The meaning of the maxims is obscure: they may once have been part of a sermon *exemplum* and summarized the moral of some involved story (cf. No. 17 below, pp. 71–2); they were probably once in verse.

XXIV

f. 46ᵇ   MORS

> f. 46ᵇ   Jam nunc in proximo mors stat ad hostium
> Et michi loquitur tale consilium
>
> .   .   .   .
>
> f. 47ᵃ   Exora filium deuote, dulciter,
> Vt nobis gaudium det eternaliter. Amen.
> Explicit materia precedens, etc.

Not in Walther; the *Supplement* (1960) records two MSS.: Laud misc. 99 (xv c.), f. 69ᵇ (**B**); Jesus College, Oxford, 39 (xv c.), p. 166 (**J**).

Ed. A. G. Rigg, *MÆ* xxxvi (1967), 249–52; thesis, i. 104–6, ii. 315–17; not previously noticed or printed.

J and **B** contain the English version of the tract *Disce mori*, discussed by Sister M. C. O'Connor, *The Art of Dying Well: the Development of the 'Ars moriendi'* (New York, 1942), p. 18 and n. It is a translation of an early *Mireour du Monde*, the probable source of the *Somme le roi*. **J** and **B** are almost certainly related: either one is copied from the other, or they share a common original. There is nothing to show whether **T** took the poem from a copy of the *Disce mori*, or whether it was originally a separate poem; the latter is more probable, as it is introduced in **J** and **B** without ceremony, and was perhaps simply inserted in the treatise as being appropriate.

The poet is addressed directly by Death on the suddenness of his approach without warning; the poet reflects on this and the inevitability of death, and the need for repentance before it is too late. The poem contains yet another example of the 'Three Sorrowful Things': see Brown, *EL XIII*, pp. 172–3.

Metre: rhythmical asclepiads in four-line stanzas.

15

f. 47ᵃ   O mors mordens aspere, yn gyle thu haste noo pere,
Nam sanos in prospere thow bryngyst to the bere,
Et tua sentencia Fallyt bothe yong and oolde,
Et fallax potencia thow makyst all vnboolde.

Index 2519; found only in **T**.

Ed. Brown, *RL XV*, No. 157. The poem acts as a coda to No. XXIV.

Metre: collateral (macaronic) Leonine hexameters.

16

f.47ᵃ   Hoo that comyȝt to an howse,
Loke he be noo thyng dongerowse,
To take seche as he fyndyȝt;
And yf he woll not do soo,
Reson agreeȝt thertoo,
To take suche as he bryngyȝt.

Index and *Suppl.* 4102. Also found in Bodley 315 (mid xv c.), f. 268ᵃ; in the Bodley version it is the second of five inscriptions copied by the scribe from the refectory at the Austin Priory at Launceston, Cornwall.

Ed. thesis, i. 107, ii. 317–18; printed from **T** in *Babees Book*, p. 35, and from the Bodley MS. by R. H. Robbins, 'Wall verses at Launceston Priory', *Archiv*, cc (1963–4), 338–43, with a full account of all the verses.

For the proverb, see Chaucer, *CT RvT*, A 4129–30; Skeat *EEP* No. 234; *ODEP* 'Take what you find'.

17

f.47ᵃ   Wyth thys bytel be he smete
That all the worle mote hyt wete,
That yevyt hys goode to hys kynne
And goth hymsylfe abeggyng.

Index and *Suppl.* 4202. Also found in: Royal 8 E. xvii (late xiii/
early xiv c.), f. 83ᵇ **(R)**; Royal 7 E. iv (late xiv c.), f. 45ᵇ **(Brom.)**;
Royal 18 B. xxiii (mid xv c.), f. 81ᵇ **(Ser.)**; Rylands Library, Latin
394 (mid xv c.), f. 18ᵇ **(L)**; Douce 295 (late xiv/early xv c.), f. 86ᵇ
(D, not in *Index)*. Delete the old *Index* reference to Douce 52.

Ed. thesis, i. 107, ii. 318–20. Printed from **T** in *Babees Book*,
p. 35 (not from **Ser.** as reported in *Index)*; from **Brom.** and **R** in
Wright, *Latin Stories*, No. xxiv, pp. 28–9, 221–2; from **R** in Brown
Register, i. 362; from **Ser.** by W. O. Ross, *Middle English Sermons*,
EETS 209 (1940), p. 90; from **L** in *Rylands Proverbs*, p. 105.

R and **L** are collections of proverbs; **Brom.** is a MS. of John of
Bromyard's *Summa Predicantium*; **Ser.** is a free English rendering
of the Bromyard sermon; **D** is a MS. of *Dives et Pauper* (see H. G.
Pfander, *Library*, 4th series, xiv (1934), 299–312). In **Brom.** and **R**
the poem is followed by, respectively, Latin and French translations:
it is probably English in origin.

The poem is the climax of a story told in full by **Brom., Ser.,** and
D: an old man is ill-treated by his children after giving them all his
goods; he pretends to have more hidden away, and is accordingly
treated well; at his death his heirs go to his treasure-chest, and find
inside a mallet and the verse. The origin of the story is discussed
by G. L. Gomme, 'A Highland Folktale', *Folklore*, i (1890), 197–206.
Similar stories include: Hoccleve, *Regement of Princes*, ed. F. J.
Furnivall, EETS, ES 72 (1897), lines 4180 ff.; 'La Houce Partie', in
E. Barbazan, *Fabliaux et contes des poètes français*, iv (Paris, 1808),
472–85; *Mery Tales and Quicke Answeres (SJB* i), No. 103; cf. also
Robert Copland, *Jyl of Breyntfords Testament*, ed. F. J. Furnivall,
Ballad Soc. 1871, 141–3, 153–5. Cf. also *Peter Idley's Instructions to
his Son*, ed. C. d'Evelyn (Boston, 1935), ii. 1140 ff., note on p. 226.

XXV

f. 47ᵃ   NOTA NOVEM PROPRIETATES VINI

Dat vinum purum ter tria comoda: primum
Vires multiplicat et viscera plena relaxat;
Confortat stomachum, cerebrum, cor dat tibi letum;
Efficit audacem, sudorem prouocat, aptat
Ingenium; tali luxus congaudet amico;
Sit mensura comes, ne violetur opus.

Walther 4078, *Sprichw.* 5020a. There are many MSS., mainly continental; for corrections to Walther's entry, see thesis or my notes in the *Supplement* to Walther (1960).

Ed. thesis, i. 107, ii. 320–1. For texts with an unspecified number of properties, see Werner, *Beiträge*, p. 158; *Flos med.* ii. 414–18 (Renzi, v. 11); *Carm. prov.*, p. 34. For another 'numerological' drinking song, cf. No. xv above.

XXVI

f. 47ᵇ   INGRATITUDO

For this Latin poem on ingratitude by Stephen Deverell, monk of Glastonbury, see below Appendix I, pp. 123–9.

18

f. 48ᵇ   WHAT EVER THOWE SAYE
                 AVYSE THE WELL

> f. 48ᵇ   Almy3ty Godde, conserue vs fram care!
> Where ys thys worle awey ywente?
>
> .   .   .   .   .
>
> f. 49ᵃ   Sende me grace both ny3t and daye;
> Whate euer thow sey, avyse the welle.
>   Explicit etc.

Index 240. Found only in **T**.

Ed. thesis, i. 111–13, ii. 325–8; *Babees Book*, pp. 356–8; Brown, *RL XV*, No. 182.

This is another poem advising caution in speech; it emphasizes the danger of betrayal by false friends, of flattery and back-biting. It has frequent echoes of the sort of moralizing common to many of the poems addressed to boys, servants, and young gentlemen edited in the *Babees Book*, and at 53–6 actually refers to the poem 'How the wise man taught his son' (*Babees Book*, pp. 48–52). For examples of other poems advising caution, see on No. 10 above.

Metre: (nine) ballade-stanzas, *ababbcbc*.

19

f. 49ᵃ   A HORSE

Here begynnyth xvᵗᵉⁿ condycyons that a goode hors schuld haue. A goode hors schuld haue iij condycyons of a man, iij of a woman, iij of a fox, iij of an hare, and iij of an asse. The iij of a man, to be prowte, boolde and hardy; the iij of a woman, to haue a faeyr breste, a fayer creste, and eesy to lepe vppon; the iij of the fox, to haue schort eerys, a feeyr tayle and a goode trott; the iij of the hare, to haue a lene hed, grete yeon and wel-rennyng-away; the iij of the asse, to haue bygge chyne, a flat leg and a goode hofe, etc.

Found also in: Lansdowne 762 (late xv c.), f. 16ᵃ (L); Book of St. Albans (1486), sig. F5ʳ (A); Porkington 10 (third quarter, xv c.), f. 188ᵇ (P); Columbia University, Plimpton Add. No. 2 (xv c.), f. 8ᵃ (Pl).
    Ed. thesis, i. 114, ii. 328–30. Printed from L in *Rel. Ant.* i. 232–3. L and A are related (see above on No. 14, p. 70); Pl agrees basically with P.
    Similar analogical descriptions of the properties of a horse are found elsewhere: twenty-five properties (*Index* and *Suppl.* 3318) in Cotton Galba E. ix, f. 113ᵇ and Balliol 354, f. 7ᵃ; eighteen in Huntington 1051 (see *HMC Report on the MSS of. . . . R. R. Hastings*, vol. i (1928), 421).

XXVII

f. 49ᵃ   TWO PROVERBS

(*a*) Omnibus amissis famam seruare memento,
    Qua semel amissa vix postea recuperabis.

(*b*) Cum facis ingressum, studeas sic esse modestus,
    Vt post regressum de te sit rumor honestus.

(*a*) Walther 13291, *Sprichw.* 20063–4, 20106. Also in Balliol 354, f. 201 (Dyboski, p. 133) and Werner, *Sprichw.*² O 62 (p. 87); two lines in Balliol, but normally only the first is given, e.g. W. Wattenbach, *Anzeiger*, xxx (1883), 124.

(*b*) Walther 3606, *Sprichw.* 4138.

XXVIII

f. 49ᵇ TRYVYTLAM DE LAUDE
    VNIVERSITATIS OXONIE

f. 49ᵇ Ad te nunc habeo verbum, O ciuitas,
    Que grandi titulo terram inhabitas

      . . . . .

f. 54ᵃ Apponas manus, O mater Oxonia,
    Vt perfruaris perhenni leticia. Amen.
    Explicit materia precedens etc.

Walther 462. Found only in **T**.

Ed. thesis, i. 115–31, ii. 333–41 (330–3). Walther records no edition, but the whole of it was transcribed by Twyne, Bodley MS. Twyne xxiv, pp. 299–307; printed by T. Hearne (ed.), *Historia vitae et regni Ricardi II* (1729), Appendix, pp. 344–58; and edited fully by H. Furneaux in *Collectanea III* (OHS xxxii, 1896), pp. 188–209. Extracts were made by Richard James, Bodley MS. James 7, pp. 84–8; by Roger Gale in an unprinted letter to Hearne (Rawlinson letters, 6, No. 40, 22 Feb. 1729); and by M. E. Marcett, *Uhtred de Boldon, Friar William Jordan and Piers Plowman* (New York, 1938), pp. 10–11.

This is the first of a group of four poems concerning the friars in the fourteenth century, the first two defending the friars, the second two attacking. The first and last concern Oxford, and xxxi is probably a reply to xxviii. The author of xxviii was Richard Tryvytlam, a Minorite and former student at Oxford; in 1350 his name was included in a list of *religiosi* in the Hereford diocese (see *BRUO* s. Trevytlam). 1–92, general praise of the University; 93–176, in her dotage Oxford encourages strife and oppresses the friars; 177–236, criticism of monks who leave their cloisters to live in luxury and who attack the friars; 237–68, they follow the heresies of William of St. Amour; there are three in particular who are embodiments of the mystical beasts of the Apocalypse: 269–364, Sene, monk of

Glastonbury; 365–448 Richard of Lincoln, Abbot of Louth Park; 449–92, Uhtred of Boldon; 493–6, conclusion.

John Seen (see *BRUO*) had incepted in theology by 1360, and seems on the whole to have had the favour of his abbot, Walter de Monyngton: see W. A. Pantin, *Documents Illustrating the Activities of the . . . English Black Monks*, iii (CS liv, 1937), Nos. 204, 322–3; Monyngton, however, was greatly concerned about the behaviour of some of his monks in Oxford (Pantin, *Documents*, Nos. 200–1, 204, 206, and 213), and Seen may well have been associated with them. The second figure, Richard de Lincoln (see *BRUO*), was Abbot of Louth Park from 1349 till after 1360; he was once under the influence of the nominalist opinions of Jean de Mirecourt and was censured by Benedict XII (the poem refers to this), but was reinstated in 1343. For Uhtred of Boldon, see Marcett, op. cit., and D. Knowles, 'The censured opinions of Uhtred of Boldon', *Proc. Brit. Acad.* xxxvii (1951), 305–42; he went to Durham College, Oxford, in 1347, eventually incepted as a doctor in 1357, and seems to have stayed as Prior of the College for about ten years more. The poem can probably be dated about 1357, when Uhtred and Seen must have been most active in the University; this date would also fit well with the possibility that xxxi is a reply to Tryvytlam.

Metre: rhythmical asclepiads, four-line stanzas.

XXIX

f. 54ᵇ   ANOTHER SONG ON BEHALF OF
THE FRIARS

f. 54ᵇ   Quis dabit ⟨meo⟩ capiti pelagus aquarum,
Vt deducant oculi fontem lacrimarum?

.   .   .   .   .

f. 56ᵃ   Wyt an O and an I, hanc litem qu⟨e⟩ sordet,
Cristus Deus dirimat et clerum concordet. Amen.
Explicit expliceat ludere scriptor eat.

Walther 16052. Found only in **T**.

Ed. thesis, i. 132–8, ii. 341–6 (330–3). Printed (with often confusing punctuation) by W. Heuser, 'With an O and an I', *Anglia*, xxvii (1904), 283–319 (text on pp. 315–19); extracts were made by Twyne (Bodley MS. Twyne xxiv, pp. 299–307).

Like the last, this poem complains about the treatment of the friars, but is concerned not with Oxford but with London. 1–64, general lament for the condition of the friars; they are attacked particularly by two 'Richards' who are trying to turn London against the friars by their sermons at Saint Paul's Cross; 65–96, justification of the doctrine of evangelical poverty; 97–150, a further account of the oppressions preached and practised by the two Richards; 151–68, the luxury and evil life of the anti-mendicants; 169–80, a prayer for concord and peace.

The first Richard was Richard Fitzralph, one of the most active of the friars' opponents; he was Archbishop of Armagh from 1346 until his death in 1360; his principal work was the *De Pauperie Salvatoris* (1356), which tried to show that the friars' mendicancy had no scriptural authority (the *De Pauperie* is partly edited by R. L. Poole, *Johannis Wycliffe* 'De dominio Divino . . .', Wyclif Soc. xvii, 1890); the poem refers to this work, and to the St. Paul's Cross sermons, delivered by Fitzralph in 1356–7; see D. Knowles, *The Religious Orders in England*, 3 vols. (1948–59), vol. ii *passim*; A. Gwynn, 'Archbishop Fitzralph and the Friars', *Studies: an Irish Quarterly Review*, xxvi (1937), 50–67, and 'Sermon-diary of Richard Fitzralph', *Proc. Royal Irish Acad.*, xliv (1937), C, 1–57. The second Richard was probably Richard Kilwyngton, Dean of St. Paul's, an active and loyal supporter of Fitzralph (see Gwynn, *Studies*, p. 62). The poem must have been written between 1357 and 1360; its author claims that he is not a friar, but intends to become one; this is probably a fiction—see my article, 'William Dunbar: the "Fenyeit Freir" ', *RES*, N.S. xiv (1963), 269–73. There are many obscurities, due mainly to the complexity of the argument, the requirements of the metre, and probably textual deficiency. The first line is from Jer. 9: 1: there are naturally many Biblical quotations. For the colophon, see C. H. Haskins, *Renaissance of the Twelfth Century* (Cambridge, Mass., 1927; repr. New York, 1957), p. 74.

Metre: four-line Goliardic stanza, with a two-line 'O-and-I' refrain; there is also internal rhyme in the four-line part of the stanza. Cf. the poem on the Council of London (1382), Wright *Pol. Poems*, i. 253–63; see Heuser, op. cit.; R. L. Greene, 'A Middle English Love Poem . . .', *MÆ* xxx (1961), 170–5; Robbins *HP*, pp. 336–7.

XXX

f. 56ª   DE ASTANTIBUS CRUCIFIXO

> f. 56ª   Est apud ecclesias autenticus hic modus et mos:
> In medio crux stat, hinc inde Maria, Johannes,
>
> .   .   .   .
>
> Sed nunquam sciui latronum nomina certa.
> Nunc scio, nunc claret via cognicionis aperta!
> et hic finis

Walther 5592. Found only in **T**.

Ed. A. G. Rigg, *Medieval Studies*, xxx (1968); thesis, i. 138, ii. 347. Copied in full by Richard James (Bodley MS. James 7, pp. 84–8), but unnoticed in modern times.

This short poem tells an amusing story at the expense of the friars: their crucifixions show not Mary and John, but a Dominican and a Franciscan; someone was puzzled at the new figures and asked a friar who they were; when told that they were a Dominican and a Franciscan, he exclaimed, 'I have always heard that two notorious thieves were crucified with Christ, but until now I did not know who they were; now I know their names for certain!'

Metre: (seventeen) hexameters with many variations from Classical Latin quantities.

XXXI

f. 56ᵇ   DE SUPERSTICIONE PHARISEORUM

> f. 56ᵇ   Ab vno de monachis amatore cleri,
> Cuius nomen nesciat exprimi vel queri
>
> .   .   .   .
>
> f. 58ᵇ   Cui, sicut digni sunt, eos commendamus,
> Et pro digno carmine te Deum laudamus.
> Explicit etc.

Walther 122. Found only in **T**.

Ed. with xxx in *Medieval Studies*, xxx (1968); thesis, i. 138–45, ii. 347–52. Extracts were made by Twyne and Richard James (cf. the last three items) but it has had no notice or attention in modern times: extract also in my *RES* article cited on xxix above.

The poem is a savage denunciation of the pharisaical friars for their arrogance and their ingratitude to the University (Oxford); the author is an anonymous monk, a supporter of the clergy. 1–8, the poem is a reply to the poem of the angry friars [this seems to me certainly to refer to Tryvytlam's poem, xxviii above]; 9–52, an elaborate comparison of the University with the sun [this picks up an image used in a less complex fashion by Tryvytlam]; 53–90, the friars ungratefully attack the secular clergy and the University; 91–134, they also attack the monks, but have at last been defeated: their ingratitude; 135–98, their arrogance, hypocrisy, and likely nemesis; 199–220, a warning to their leader, a plea for humility, and a final condemnation.

The poem refers to the 'recent' death of Gaveston (1312) and suppression of the Templars (1313), and Richard James therefore dated the poem '*tempore* Ed. 2'; however, the correspondences with Tryvytlam's poem seem to me overwhelming: the triumphant tone may refer to the failure of the delegation to Avignon led by the Minorite Roger Conway *c.* 1357.

Metre: Goliardic (220 lines) rhyming in couplets.

XXXII

f. 58ᵇ   NON-CELEBRANT PRIESTS

Beda: Quod sacerdos qui est sine peccato mortali et in bono proposito et non celebrat, cum habeat sacerdos copiam celebrandi quantum in ipso est, sanctam trinitatem priuat gloria, angelos in celesti Jerusalem manentes leticia, homines in terra laborantes beneficio et gracia, animas in purgatorio detentas patrocinio et venia.

I have not found this note in the works of Bede. It was added some time later than xxxi; it may or may not have been intended as a further accusation against the friars.

20

f. 58ᵇ   EASTER

Yn Marche aftyr the fyrste C
The nextt pryme tell yee me;
The thyrdde Sonday full, ywys,
Estyr Day sykyr hitt ys.
Pri pri pri di di di pas cha ffi

Index and *Suppl.* 1502. Also found in: Bodley Misc. lat. e 22 (1416–50), end of roll (**M1**); CUL, Ee 4. 35, pt. 1 (early xv c.), f. 5ᵃ (**E**); CUL, Ff 6. 8 (added in xvi c.), f. 3ᵇ (**F**); Magdalene College, Cambridge, 13 (early xvi c.), f. 9ᵃ (**M**); T.C.C. O.1.57 (xv c.), f. 4ᵃ (**T2**); Royal 2 A. xvii (added in xvi c.), f. 5ᵃ (**R**); Lambeth Palace 545 (early xvi c.), f. 2ᵃ (**L**); Brough Hall (xv c.) with a Latin version (**Br**); Harley 3810 (xv c.), f. 52ᵇ (two copies: **H1, H2**); Digby 88 (xv c.), f. 82ᵇ (**D**); Royal 8 F. xii (xv c.), f. 43ᵃ (**R2**); Sloane 747 (late xv c.), f. 46ᵃ (**S**); Brooke *Horae BVM* (added xv c.) (**Bk**); Balliol 354 (xvi c.), f. 6ᵇ (**B**); BN lat. 3638, f. 75ᵃ (first couplet only). **B** is not in *Index* or *Suppl.*

Ed. thesis, i. 146, ii. 353–6. Printed as follows: from **F** by Robbins *SL*, No. 70; from **T2** by James *Catalogue*, iii. 55; from **R** by E. Bishop in *Lay-folk's Prayer book*, EETS 109 (1897), Introd., p. xlix; from **L** by M. R. James and C. Jenkins, *Catalogue of MSS . . . of Lambeth Palace*, 2 vols. (1930–2), p. 748; from **Br** in *HMC Third Report* (1872), p. 255; from **Bk** in *Catalogue of the MSS . . . of Thomas Brooke*, 2 vols. (1891), i. 266. A full account of these poems is given in my article, 'The letter *C* and the date of Easter', *ELN* v (1967), 1–5.

C is the 7 March; the *pryme* is the New Moon. All MSS. except **T, E**, and **Bk** add the proviso that, if the New Moon falls on a Sunday, that Sunday should be counted as the first of the three. With this proviso, the poem's instructions concur with those of the Nicene decree (for an explanation, see my article or thesis). The mnemonic is usually found in calendars or *Horae*; many MSS. make complete nonsense of the instructions, and there are great differences between versions.

XXXIII

f. 59ª   DESCRIPTIO NORTHFOLCHIÆ

f. 59ª   Exiit edictum ab Augusto Cesare,
          Qui mittens nuncios iussit describere

                    .   .   .   .   .

f. 62ª   Dictorum corrigat virorum opera
          Aut simul destruat gentem cum patria.

Walther 6074. Also found in: T.C.C. O.2.45 (xiii c., after 1248),
p. 340 (**T2**); Cotton Titus A. xx (xiii c.), f. 165ᵇ (**Ti**); Rawlinson
B. 214 (xv c.), f. 180ª (**R**); Bodley 487 (late xv c.), f. 19ᵇ (**B**); BM
Addit. 11619 (xiv c.), f. 277ᵇ (**Bm**: fragment only, containing lines
1–14: f. 277 is the last leaf in the MS.).

Ed. thesis, i. 146–56, ii. 356–70. Ed. from **T**, **T2**, and **Ti** only by
T. Wright, *Early Mysteries and Other Latin Poems* (1838), pp. 93–
106; an extract was made from Wright by K. P. Harrington,
Medieval Latin (Boston, 1925; repr. Chicago, 1962), pp. 511–13.
A translation (very inaccurate) was made by R. Howlett in *Norfolk
Antiquarian Miscellany*, ed. W. Rye, ii (1883), 364–82.

T differs from all other texts in the addition of two more stories,
four lines, and the displacing of thirteen lines. **R** and **Ti** are very
closely related: see also on No. iv above. Evidence for the loss of at
least two more MSS. of the poem is found in Bale (see thesis, ii.
357–8). A naïve reply to the *Descriptio*, entitled the *Impugnatio
Descriptionis Northfolchie* (contained in **Ti** and **R**), was written by
one John of St. Omer (ed. T. Wright, op. cit., and translated by
R. Howlett). The *Impugnatio* was clearly not based on an extant
MS. of the *Descriptio*, as supposed by Wright, and therefore, as it
follows the wording of the *Descriptio* closely, affords independent
textual evidence.

The poem is a scurrilous but not very serious attack on the people
of Norfolk; according to John of St. Omer, its author was a monk of
Peterborough, who presumably wrote in the early thirteenth century.
His attack is really a frame for stories illustrating stupidity (see
W. A. Clouston, *The Book of Noodles* (1888)): 1–43, Caesar is told
by one of his messengers that Norfolk is the worst province in the
world: wheat will not grow there and is in fact detested by the inhabi-
tants; 44–97, the people once used the seal of a charter of manu-
mission as a candle, and so lost their freedom; 98–103, tenants are
obliged to pay money in place of their excrement; 104–8, if asked the

way, they reply 'Go as the crow flies'; 109–13, they ride to market carrying sacks on their backs to save their beasts; 114–30, they get very drunk on an inferior beer; 131–43, to save money on entertaining, they buy one loaf between them, which they keep until it goes bad; then they eat it; 144–7, if someone calls, they say 'We are not at home'; 148–73, a man once tried to sell some honey which his dog had eaten and been forced to vomit; 174–81, a farmer found a beetle, which he took home to eat; 182–99, a yokel found a large toad, which he insisted was a partridge; 200–25, a Norfolk man forced his pet crow to excrete a coin which it had swallowed; 226–59, their vices in general; conclusion.

Analogues for some of the stories can be found in collections such as Wright's *Latin Stories*, Owlglass literature, *Shakespeare Jest Books* (*SJB*), etc.; many can be traced back into folklore: see thesis *passim*.

Metre: rhythmical asclepiads; stanzas of varying lengths.

XXXIV

f. 62ᵃ   VERSUS DE QUATUOR
COMPLEXIONIBUS

f. 62ᵃ   Largus, amans, hilaris, ridens rubeique coloris;
Cantans, carnosus, satis audax atque benignus.

.   .   .   .   .

Parum appetit, quia frigidus est;
Parum potest, quia siccus est.

Walther 10131, *Sprichw.* 13474; L. Thorndike and P. Kibre, *Catalogue of Incipits of Medieval Scientific Writings in Latin* (1963), col. 811. The verses were very popular and there are many MSS.

Ed. thesis, i. 156–7, ii. 370–2; for further references, see Walther.

In **T** each complexion, Sanguine, Choleric, Phlegmatic, and Melancholic, has a verse couplet and two lines of prose; most of the references in Walther refer to versions with couplets only, but see also Balliol 354, f. 178ᵇ, and L. Thorndike, 'Unde versus', *Traditio*, xi (1955), 179–80. There is also a longer version, in which the couplets precede longer stanzas: see *Flos med.* i. 1172–97, ii. 1690–1715 (Renzi, i. 483–4, v. 48–9); *Regimen sanitatis*, 260–85. The two English versions (Robbins, *SL*, Nos. 76 and 77) translate the couplets only, with or without prose; one of the English versions is edited by

Person, *CMEL*, No. 58, with some misleading notes. The more succinct couplet version is probably older than the stanzaic one.

Metre: mixed Leonine hexameters.

XXXV

f. 62ᵃ   Help God, and haue all.
          Det Deus auxilium, et fiat omne suum.

Walther, *Sprichw*. 5502. Both Latin and English are found in Douce 52 (*Douce Proverbs*, p. 45); English only in *Rylands Proverbs*, p. 96. *Help* is subjunctive; the redundant *and* suggests that the English is a translation of the Latin.

Metre: Leonine hexameter.

XXXVI

f. 62ᵃ Petrus eram, quem petra tegit, dictusque Commestor,
         Nunc comedor; viuus docui, nec cesso docere
         Mortuus, vt dicat qui me vidit incineratum
         'Quod sumus, iste fuit; erimus quandoque quod hic est.'

Walther 14050. This didactic 'mortality epitaph' was extremely popular.

Ed. thesis, i. 157, ii. 372. See also Aeneas Sylvius, *Epitaphia virorum illustrium* (Bodley shelf-mark Douce A 337, sig. B 5ᵛ, after 1502), ed. L. Bertalot in *Collectanea variae doctrinae Leoni S. Olschki* (Munich, 1921), pp. 1–28 (text on p. 13).

XXXVII

f. 62ᵃ   INTERPRETACIO NOMINIS WILLELMI

         Vir validus, iustus, largus, liberalis, electus,
         Lumine mundatus, virtute sanctificatus.

Walther 20428: not found elsewhere. It was perhaps composed for a patron.

Metre: single-sound Leonine couplet.

XXXVIII

f. 62^b THE EUCHARIST

Nos qui viuificat panis celi benedicat;
Sit nobis gratum corpus de virgine natum;
Pane salutari det nos Cristus saciari;
Pane Dei viuo saluemur ab hoste nociuo;
Vera resurgentis caro nos purget labe mentis;
A baratro tristi nos conseruet caro Cristi;
Misteriis sacris repleant nos verba salutis;
Sacra carne Jesu saluemur mortis ab esu;
Cristi cara caro nos sistat in ethere claro;
Salue, salus, virtus, benediccio, gloria, ympnus.

Walther 12264. Also in Balliol 235, f. 2^b, with some different lines.
Ed. thesis, i. 157–8, ii. 373. Not previously printed.
Metre: Leonine hexameters.

XXXIX

f. 62^b FORTUNE

O Fortuna leuis, cui vis, scito, das bona que vis;
Sed cui vis que vis, auferet hora brevis.
Promouet in primis Fortuna virum, sed in ymis
Huic aduersatur, cum velle suum variatur,
Crescentis lune seu preterit omnis ymago;
De spe Fortune labilis illud ago:
Ludus Fortune variatur ymagine lune—
Crescit, decrescit, in eodem sistere nescit.

Walther 12655, *Sprichw.* 19470 (a misleading entry). Also found in:
Codex Buranus (xiii c.), f. 48^b (**B**); Basel UB. A. XI. 67 (xv c.), f. 184^a
(**B1**); T.C.C. R.5.32 (xv c.), f. 104^b (**T2**); Harley 200 (xiv c.), f. 143^a
(**H**); Harley 3362 (xvi c.), f. 7^b (**H2**); Magdalen College, Oxford,
109 (xv c.), f. 108^a (**O**); Lincoln Cathedral 209 (xiv. c), f. 94^b (**L**);
Vienna 4119 (xvi c.), f. 35^b (**V**).

Ed. thesis, i. 158, ii. 373–4, and from all MSS. except **V** by Hilka and Schumann, *Carm. Bur.* I. 1. 36–7 (Notes, II. 30)—my edition was based on their readings. The last two lines of **T** (in a slightly different form) are also in **H2**, a fact not noticed by Hilka and Schumann, whose edition also misread *preterit* as *protegit*. Versions differ in the number of lines. See also H. Walther, '*Rota Fortunæ* im lateinischen Verssprichwort des Mittelalters', *Mittellateinisches Jahrbuch* i (1964), 48–58.

Metre: mixed Leonine hexameters.

XL

THE *AGNUS DEI*

Balsamus et munda cera cum crismatis vnda
Efficiunt agnum; cur ⟨munu⟩s do tibi magnum,
Fonte velut natum, per mistica sanctificatum?
Fulgura desursum depellit ⟨et⟩ omne malignum;
Pregnans saluatur, partus sine 'Ve' liberatur;
Portatus munde saluat a fluctibus vnde.

Walther 2058, Chevalier 24055, Leyser p. 1008. There are at least 43 MSS.

Ed. thesis, i. 158, ii. 374–5. Printed frequently: e.g., Johannes de Fordun, *Scotichronicon*, VIII, Ch. xxxiii, 2 vols. (Edinburgh, 1759, i. 483–4); B. Hauréau, 'Mss. du Mont-Cassin', *Journal des Savants* (1885), p. 427; *Flos med.* i, 1845–55, ii. 2873–83 (Renzi, i. 505, v. 84). Most versions have more lines than **T**.

The verse accompanied the gift of an artificial lamb sent by Pope Urban V (I have seen no version which supports Leyser's Innocent V) to the Emperor, after peace had been brought about by a miraculous parchment inscribed with the *Agnus Dei*.

Metre: Leonine hexameters.

21

f. 62ᵇ   WHO CAN NOT WEPE COM
                  LERNE OF ME

   f. 62ᵇ   Sodenly afrayd,
                 Halfe wakyng, halfe slepyng,
                 And gretly dysmayd,
                 A woman sate wepyng.
                 Wyth fauour yn here face far passyng my reson

                    .   .   .   .   .

   f. 63ᵃ   Who can not wepe—thys ys the lay.
                 And wyth that wordys schee vanyschyd away.
                              Finis

Index and *Suppl.* 4189. Also found in Rylands Library 395 (early
xv c.), f. 120ᵃ (**R**).

   Ed. thesis, i. 159–60, ii. 376–8. Printed from **T** in *EEL*, pp. 144–5,
and Furnivall *Hymns*, pp. 126–7; from **R** by S. E. Brydges, *Censura
literaria*, 2nd edn. (1815), x. 173–4, by Greene, *EEC*, No. 161 (with
readings from **T**) and by Brown, *RL XV*, No. 9. In **T** the poem is
written partly as prose.

   The poet sees the Virgin weeping, with her dead son in her lap;
she rebukes the poet for his failure to weep at the death of his father
(and brother), her son: she can teach him to weep; she vanishes.
For other occurrences of this lesson, see the 'De arte lacrimandi', ed.
R. M. Garrett, *Anglia*, xxxii (1909), 269–94, and 'O thou with Heart
of Stone', *RL XV*, No. 8. The opening lines are obscure: from the
end of the poem we gather that the poet has been dreaming, so
halfe wakyng should probably refer not to the Virgin but to the poet:
sate may be an error for *sawe y*.

   The poem is remarkably similar both in its stanza-scheme and
sentiment to 'Wofully araid' (Skelton, i. 141–3; Brown, *RL XV*,
No. 103; R. T. Davies, *Medieval English Lyrics* (1963), No. 106):
there are frequent verbal echoes (see thesis) and, indeed, the burden
of 'Wofully araid' would fit this poem. Skelton's authorship of
'Wofully araid' is denied by Brown, *RL XV*, pp. 325–6 (followed by
Davies, p. 347); it has not, however, previously been noticed that
Skelton makes jocular use of 'Who can not wepe' 12–15 in the
'Garlande of Laurell' (Skelton, i. 361–427), lines 1038–40, addressed
to 'mastres Gertrude Statham'. If he knew 'Who can not wepe'

well enough to use it there, he might well have actually adapted it as 'Wofully araid', a monologue of Christ from the Cross.

Metre: after the introduction, four nine-line stanzas *aaaabbbcc*, of which the *a*-lines have twelve syllables, the *b*-lines six, and the *c*-lines usually eight.

XLI

f. 63ª   DE PETRO DE GAVERSTONE

f. 63ª Vexilla regni prodeunt; fulget cometa comitum—
Comes dico Lancastrie, qui domuit indomitum

. . . . .

Te, summa Deus trinitas, oramus prece sedula,
Fautores Petri destruas et conteras per secula. Amen.

Walther 20284, Chevalier 21483. Not found elsewhere.

Ed. thesis, i. 160–1, ii. 378–81. Printed with a translation by Wright, *Pol. Songs*; pp. 258–9; transcribed by Hearne, *Collections*, x, 1 June 1729.

The poem is a skilful parody of the hymn *Vexilla regis* by Venantius Fortunatus (*OBMLV*, No. 55): for similar parodies, see below on No. XLII. It is a song of triumphant jubilation at the execution in 1312 of Edward II's widely detested favourite Piers Gaveston at the hands of Thomas, Count of Lancaster. The best contemporary authority, with which Nos. XLI and XLII agree in many details, is the *Vita Edwardi Secundi* (*Chronicles of the reigns of Edward I and II*, ed. W. Stubbs, 2 vols. (RS lxxvi, 1882–3), ii. 155–294). Both this and the following poem must have been written shortly after Gaveston's death: Thomas of Lancaster (executed 1322) is clearly still alive, and XLII. 25 refers to the *edes Petri*, probably the temporary resting-place of Gaveston's body in Oxford, where it remained until 1314.

Metre: adaptation of quantitative iambic dimeters into fourteen rhythmical sixteen-syllable iambic lines rhyming in couplets (disyllabic and trisyllabic rhyme): the change from quantity to rhythm has produced some curious stresses.

XLII

f. 63ᵃ ANOTHER POEM ON GAVESTON

f. 63ᵃ Pange, lingua, necem Petri qui turbauit Angliam,
Quem rex amans super omnem pretulit Cornubiam

. . . . .

f. 63ᵇ Qui fecerunt Petrum mori cum suis carminibus;
Amodo sit pax et plausus in Anglorum finibus. Amen.

Walther 13617, Chevalier 14501. Not found elsewhere.

Ed. thesis, i. 161–2, ii. 378–82. Printed with translation by Wright, *Pol. Songs*, pp. 259–61; transcribed by Hearne, *Collections*, x, 1 June 1729. Written as prose in **T**.

This parodies the *Pange lingua gloriosi* by Venantius Fortunatus (*OBMLV*, No. 54), and also celebrates enthusiastically the death of Gaveston: see above on No. XLI. For other parodies of these hymns, see Walther 20283–5 and 13611–17; many are secular, including ones on the Siege of Parma (1248), the Hussites, and the death of Richard, Count of Pembroke; see further Lehmann, *Parodie*, p. 3. One of the most notable parodies of the *Pange lingua* in the present context is the lament for Gaveston's executioner, Thomas of Lancaster (d. 1322), found in an 'office' in his honour (Wright, *Pol. Songs*, pp. 268–72.) The two poems in **T** are certainly the most skilful of all the parodies, and pun with remarkable facility.

Metre: adaptation of quantitative catalectic trochaic tetrameters (trochaic septenarii) into the rhythmical fifteen-syllable line (8p+ 7pp), the metre of the *Apparebit repentina* (Norberg, p. 114); there are ten three-line stanzas with trisyllabic or disyllabic rhyme. As in XLI there are many curious stresses.

XLIII

f. 63ᵇ THREE PROVERBS

(*a*) Munera pauca seni, puero des ac mulieri,
Nam senex moritur, puer immemor, femina mutat.

(*b*) Si bona vina cupis, ff quinque serua in illis:
Forcia, formosa, fragrancia, frigida, frisca.

(c) Quatuor ex sompno generantur meridiano:
Febris, pigricies, capitis dolor atque catarrus.

(a) Walther, *Sprichw.* 15680 (without **T**). Ed. thesis, ii. 382; cf. below,
No. *20 (iii), Appendix II, pp. 145–6.

(b) Walther 17635, *Sprichw.* 28257 (without **T**). Ed. thesis, ii. 382–3;
see also *Regimen sanitatis*, 36–7, *Flos med.* i. 239–40, ii. 408–9 (Renzi
i. 452, v. 11), P. Lehmann, 'Skandinavische Reisefrüchte', *Nordisk
Tidskrift för Bok- och Biblioteksväsen*, xxii (1935), 103–31 (text on
p. 106): versions differ slightly.

(c) Walther 15308, 18298, *Sprichw.* 23678, 29779 (without **T**). Ed.
thesis, ii. 383; see also *Regimen sanitatis*, 15–17, *Flos med.* i. 143–5,
ii. 246–8 (Renzi i. 449, v. 7)—these versions have three lines.
Werner, *Sprichw.²* A 153, p. 25, has a single line version.

XLIV

f. 64ᵃ   TANCRED OF SALERNE

f. 64ᵃ   Tancredus Princeps Salermitanus, vir mitis quidem ac
benigni ingenii, si modo in senecta manus suas aman-
cium sanguinem

.   .   .   .   .

f. 68ᵃ   sera penitencia ductus publico ac doloroso Saler-
mitanorum funere in eodem sepulcro sepiliri ambos
fecit.
     Per Leonardum Aretinum de Italico in Latinum
translatum.

This Latin translation of *Decameron* iv. 1 has most recently been
printed (from a fifteenth-century incunabulum) by H. G. Wright,
*Early English Versions of the Tale of Guiscardo and Ghismonda . . .
from the 'Decameron'*, EETS 205 (1937), pp. 102–28. See also D. M.
Manni, *Istoria del 'Decamerone'* (Florence, 1742), pp. 246–56.
Between 1470 and 1500 seventeen editions of the translation were
published (*Gesamtkatalog der Wiegendrucke*, 7 vols., A–Eig (Leipzig,
1925–), Nos. 5626–42); from the texts I have seen (Wright,
Manni, and *GKW* No. 5636, Bodley shelf-mark Auct. N 5.9) it

seems likely that **T**, though corrupt and deficient, is closer to the original than any: see thesis, ii. 383–4.

This extremely popular story tells how Tancred's daughter, Sigismunda, was widowed early but because of her father's inordinate love for her was unable to find another husband; she fell in love with one of the servants, Guiscardo, and they managed to meet and make love: Guiscardo entered her room through a secret tunnel. One day Tancred was in Sigismunda's room; he fell asleep under a cover, but awoke to hear the couple making love on the bed. He had Guiscardo arrested and killed, and sent his heart on a platter to Sigismunda, who committed suicide. A large part of the story, whose popularity survived for five centuries, is taken up by Sigismunda's defence of her love for a lowly servant.

The translation into Latin was made by Leonardo Bruni of Arezzo in 1436 or 1438 (both dates are found in texts of a letter from Bruni: see Wright, op. cit., p. lvi, n. 4; Manni, p. 247), and is thus the latest datable entry made by **T**. The Latin is 'humanistic' and involved, and seems to have given the scribe much trouble.

XLV

f. 68ª   NATIVITY HYMN

f. 68ª   Parit virgo filium regali stirpe Dauid.

Puer natus in Bethlem
Vnde gaudet Jerusalem   Cristus illuminauit

.   .   .   .   .

Cognouit bos et asinus
Quod puer erat Dominus   Cristus illuminauit

Chevalier 32017, 15784–7. A large number of MSS.

Ed. thesis, i. 163, ii. 384–6. See also: *AH* i. 163–4, xx. 99; H. A. Daniel, *Thesaurus hymnologicus*, 5 vols. in 2 (Halle and Leipzig, 1841–56), i. 334; K. E. P. Wackernagel, *Das deutsche Kirchenlied* (Stuttgart, 1841), No. 62; J. C. von Zabüsnig, *Katholische Kirchengesänge*, 3 vols. (Augsburg, 1822), i. 230; J. M. Neale, *Hymni ecclesiae e breviariis* (1851), p. 63; R. C. Trench, *Sacred Latin Poetry* (1849), pp. 93–4. Texts differ enormously in the number and order of stanzas (see thesis); I have seen no other version with the *Cristus illuminauit* refrain. The hymn is an undistinguished celebration of the Nativity.

Metre: rhythmical equivalent of the iambic dimeter.

22

f. 68ᵇ   BEWARE OF SWERYNG BY THE
                    MASSE

> f. 68ᵇ   Y concell yow, both more and lasse,
> Be ware of sweryng by the masse.
>
> .   .   .   .   .
>
> For when erth hath coueryde thy face,
> Then all that ys turnyd as hyt wasse.

Index 3424. Found also in Balliol 354 (xvi c.), f. 230ᵃ (**B**). Ed. thesis, i. 163–4, ii. 386–7. Printed from **T** by Greene *EEC*, No. 331 (with readings from **B**); from **B** by Flügel, 'Liedersammlungen', pp. 263–4, Dyboski, pp. 42–3. **B** omits sts. v–vi, in place of which it has a stanza not in **T**. It was on the basis of this poem that Greene postulated a relationship between **T** and **B**, but see my notes in *N. & Q.* ccxi (1966), 324–30.

The poem cautions against the use of the word 'Mass' in oaths: the Mass is of great dignity, and in it lies man's hope of salvation; the man who swears by the Mass is doomed to hell-fire. For sermons against swearing, see G. R. Owst, *Literature and Pulpit in Medieval England*, 2nd edn. (1961), pp. 414–25; Chaucer, *CT Pars. T.*, X. 586–99; *Pard. T.*, C. 472–5, 629–59: for another poem on the subject, see Person, *CMEL*, No. 26. Poems on the subject of, and in praise of, the Mass are to be found in *Lay-Folk's Mass Book*, ed. T. F. Simmons, EETS 71 (1879).

Metre: four-line stanzas *aaaa*; the first couplet is the burden.

XLVI

f. 68ᵇ   WORLDLY VANITY

f. 68ᵇ   Si tibi pulcra domus, si splendida mensa, quid inde?
        Si tibi sponsa decens, si sit generosa, quid inde?
        Si fueris fortis, pulcher diuesve, quid inde?
        Si prior aut abbas, si rex, si papa, quid inde?
        Que sunt sub celo, si sint tua cuncta, quid inde?
        Tam cito pretereunt hec omnia quod nichil inde:
        Sola manent merita, q⟨uia⟩ glorificaberis inde.

Walther 15819, *Sprichw.* 29270a. Walther lists twenty-three different
incipits for the poem (s. *Quid inde*): there is clearly a great number of
MSS.

Ed. thesis, i. 164–5, ii. 387–8. See L. Bertalot, *Humanistisches
Studienheft eines Nürnberger Scholaren aus Pavia* (1460) (Berlin,
1910), pp. 100–3; W. Wattenbach, *NA* xviii (1892–3), 515.

The fullest (though not the earliest extant) version is one in which
we have a dialogue between Dives, such as the one we have here, and
Pauper, who comments similarly on the transitoriness of misfortune;
another version (*Rel. Ant.* i. 57–8) alternates Dives and Pauper
lines. The most common has the Dives part only, as does T—it was
more usual to interpret the transitoriness of earthly fortune in a
pessimistic way, as does the earliest extant text, which, however,
implies a dialogue by beginning *Dives ait.* . . . The frequent MS.
attribution to Bernard of Cluny is probably due simply to the gloomy
theme of the *De Contemptu Mundi.*

Metre: hexameters.

23

f. 69ᵃ   ENGLISH PROVERBS

f. 69ᵃ   Salamon seyth ther is none accorde
        Ther euery man wuld be a lord

            .   .   .   .   .

        Grace passyth golde and precyous stone;
        God schall be God when golde is gone.

Index and *Suppl.* 3170 (for ff. 70ᵃ–77ᵃ read f. 69ᵃ). This arrangement of proverbs is only in **T**.

Ed. thesis, i. 165–6, ii. 388–91; Person, *CMEL* No. 59.

Most of the proverbs here can be found elsewhere in the main collections of Middle English proverbs: see thesis for references and elucidations.

Metre: (fifteen) couplets.

XLVII

f. 69ᵇ   THE SOUL IN HELL (by John the Deacon)

f. 69ᵇ   Quod anima potest esse in inferno et cruciatus inferni non sentire: Notandum quod non legitur beati Gregorii precibus Trayani

.   .   .   .   .

cunctos equaliter non valet exurere, nam vniuscuiusque quantum meruerit culpa, iusto Dei iudicio tantum sencietur et pena.

This passage is taken from John the Deacon's *Vita S. Gregorii* (*PL* lxxv, 59–242), II, Ch. 44 (cols. 105–6). John (d. before 882) tells the familiar story of how Gregory (!) was present when Trajan, on his way to war, was asked by a widow to do justice on behalf of her murdered son; despite his haste Trajan did so, and Gregory was so impressed that he wept for Trajan's soul and saved him from hell. There were various religious objections to the redemption, mainly based on Gregory, *Dialogues* IV, Ch. xliv (*PL* lxxvii, 401–5), because the text of praying for one's enemies (Matt. 5: 44) applied only to the possibility of repentance (2 Tim. 2: 25). John notes, however, that Gregory did not pray for Trajan, but wept. He then goes on to explain in this passage how God in his mercy can grant redemption to those detained in hell: there are various types and degrees of fire in hell (so also Gregory, loc. cit.). The story of Trajan's redemption is also told by Langland, *Piers Plowman*, B-text xi, 135 ff. (C-text xiii, 75 ff.).

XLVIII

f. 69ᵇ SAINT HILDA AND WHITBY ABBEY

f. 69ᵇ   Jam, mera Clio, sona, iam sis ad carmina prona;
Psalle, precor, vitam multis plus melle cupitam

.   .   .   .   .

f. 76ᵇ   Grandis vindicta fuit a Bega benedicta
Istis conflicta; sic est sua cura relicta.

Not in Walther. Found only in **T**, but another MS. existed in the eighteenth century.

Ed. thesis, i. 167–85, ii. 393–422. Not previously noticed.

The poem is in two parts: the first (1–551) celebrates at length the life and virtues of St. Hilda of Whitby, and adds the story of Cædmon's miraculous inspiration; this section is based primarily on Bede, but with the addition of two legends (the ridding of the abbey of serpents and predatory birds) told in other lives, such as that in *NLA*, ii. 29–33, by John of Tynemouth (though Tynemouth was certainly not the source of the poem), and some details which may have been the invention of the poet himself. The second part (552–609, in Leonine single-sound couplets) tells of the refoundation of the abbey by the ex-soldier Reinfrid, under the patronage of William Percy; the second part is very oblique and obscure in its narrative, but it is clear that the poet was not following any of the known versions of the refoundation of the abbey (Symeon of Durham, 2 vols., RS lxxv, 1882–5; *Whitby Cartulary*, ed. J. C. Atkinson, Surtees Soc., lxix, lxxii, 1878–9, including also the *Memorial of Benefactions* and the *Chronicle of Stephen of Whitby*); many of the details in the second half (particularly concerning the translation of St. Hilda's relics to Glastonbury) are found only in otherwise un-related material, such as William of Malmesbury's historical works, and in modern writers such as Leland or John Burton, *Monasticon Eboracense* (1758), who quotes (p. 69) from a Whitby Register belonging to the Cholmley family and not now extant. Other important evidence is found in Bodley MSS. Dodsworth 118, f. 87, and 159, f. 115ᵇ, which actually quote the last lines of the poem, though it is almost impossible that Dodsworth knew **T**. The poem in fact is an invaluable source for early Whitby history, or at least for the documentation of the history.

The poem shows some clumsy versification, but is not devoid of rhetorical ornament. In this poem the damage to the end of the MS. becomes very apparent, and many lines are deficient.

Metre: 1–551, Leonine hexameters; 552–609, single-sound Leonine couplets.

XLIX

f. 76ᵇ   CONVENTUAL DIET by Abbot Henry de Blois

See below, Appendix I, pp. 129–30.

L

f. 77ᵃ   LETTER FROM COLOGNE (9 June 1434)
from Abbot Nicholas Frome

See below, Appendix I, pp. 130–9.

LI

f. 78ᵇ   Tu Jesus in missa quociens audis Marie
Tu Jesus in missa quociens audisve Maria
Et flectis genua, Johannes dat tibi papa
Et veniam scelerum viginti nempe dierum

Walther 19484. The *papa* is probably Pope John XXIII (1410–15).

LII

f. 79ᵃ   HISTORIA DE SANCTA CRUCE

f. 79ᵃ   Postquam Adam expulsus est eodem die [de] Para-
diso propter peccatum, dum clamaret [pro] miseri-
cordia Domini, indutus

·   ·   ·   ·   ·

f. 82ᵃ   dicitur Caluaria, et in ea crucif[ixerunt] Jesum Cristum
in salutem omnium cred[entium, cui sit] honor et
gloria in secula seculorum.

For editions of the Latin History of the Cross, see W. Meyer, 'Das
Geschichte des Kreuzholtes vor Christus', *Abhandlungen der philoso-
phisch-philologischen Classe der königlich bayerischen Akademie der
Wissenschaften* (Munich), xvi (1882), part ii, 103–65 (text on pp. 131–
49); H. Suchier, *Denkmäler provenzalischer Literatur und Sprache*
(Halle, 1883), pp. 165–200, 525–8; C. Horstman, 'Nachträge zu den
Legenden', *Archiv*, lxxix (1887), 411–70 (text on pp. 465–70). The
text of **T** is very deficient because of damage and the inattention of
the scribe; generally speaking, it does not differ substantially from
other versions.

The legend tells of Adam's weariness after the Fall, his abstention
from Eve, the visit of Seth to the Garden, where he is given three
grains from the tree and shown a vision of Abel in hell and of the
infant Christ. Seth returns to Adam, who laughs for the only time
in his life; when Adam dies, Seth places the grains in his mouth: they
are the promised 'oil of mercy'. The grains grow into trees, are trans-
planted by Moses to Mount Tabor, and discovered by David: the
trees grow together into a single stock; Solomon cuts the tree down,
but the beam miraculously will not fit in the building of the temple;
a woman named Maximilla catches fire when she sits on the beam,
and is martyred for calling on Christ. It is thrown into a sheep-dip,
and miraculously cures people; it is used as a bridge, but the Sibyl
refuses to soil it with her feet. Finally it is used in the Crucifixion.

See E. C. Quinn, *The quest of Seth for the oil of life* (Chicago,
1962), rev. J. M. Evans, *MÆ* xxxiv (1965), 85–8; A. S. Napier,
History of the Holy Rood-tree, EETS 103 (1894), pp. xxxi–xxxiv;
Legends of the Holy Rood, ed. R. Morris, EETS 46 (1871); *SEL*,
pp. 167–74; *Cursor Mundi*, Parts I and II, ed. R. Morris, EETS, 57,
59 (1874–5), ll. 1237–42, 6301–68, 7973–8262, 8757–8976—the first
part is edited by J. A. W. Bennett and G. V. Smithers, *Early Middle
English Verse and Prose*, with Glossary by Norman Davis (1966),
pp. 184–95, Notes pp. 366–70. For the sources of the legend (in this
form, twelfth-century), see Meyer, op. cit.

LIII

f. 82ᵇ [Fuit quidam] rex, nomine Tiries, qui quandam [puellam n]omine Pilam, filiam cuiusdam molendi[na]rii
nomine Atus

.   .   .   .   .

f. 84ᵃ vbi adhuc relacione quorundam quedam diabolice
machinaciones ebullire videntur, etc.

The medieval Life of Pilate has not been edited, but the version found
in **T** corresponds almost exactly to part of the chapter 'De passione
Domini' in Jacobus a Voragine's *Legenda Aurea*, Ch. liii, pp. 231–5.
For a discussion of the relationship between the *Legenda* version,
T, and a text in Bodley MS. 90, f. 105ᵃ, see thesis, ii. 434–6. At the
end of the story the *Legenda* and Bodley add a passage taken almost
verbatim from Peter Comestor's *Historia Scholastica* (*PL* cxcviii),
1680.

A certain girl called Pila, daughter of a miller, Atus, had a son by
the king; she called the child *Pil-atus*, and when he was three she
sent him to the king. When he began to grow up, Pilate killed the
king's legitimate son out of envy, and was sent to Rome as part of
the annual tribute; in Rome he killed the son of the King of France.
The Romans, amazed at his wickedness and capacity for survival,
sent him as governor to the intransigent island of Panthos (whence
his surname Pontius). He was so successful there that Herod made
him his deputy, in charge of Judea; Pilate amassed great wealth
there, unknown to Herod, and went to Rome and purchased the
lands which he had before held as a tenant: this was the cause of the
enmity between Pilate and Herod (an alternative reason is also given,
derived from the *Historia Scholastica*, Ch. xxviii, 1551). After Christ's
Crucifixion, Pilate feared Tiberius's anger and sent a messenger to
Rome to explain the facts (the Latin *Life* forgets this messenger, but
see *SEL* p. 703). In the meantime Tiberius had fallen ill with leprosy,
and sent Valesianus to Jerusalem to bring him the famous Healer.
Valesianus met a disciple of Christ, Veronica, who told him of the
Crucifixion, and offered to cure Tiberius with her veil, which had
been impressed with Christ's face. When Tiberius had been cured,
he sent for Pilate, but as the latter was wearing Christ's tunic (made
by the Virgin) Tiberius was unable to be angry; eventually Pilate
was forced to remove the tunic, and was imprisoned and committed

suicide. His body was rejected, with great commotions, by the rivers Tiber and Rhône; eventually he was buried at Lausanne, where devilish emanations are still seen.

For the popular stories on the death of Pilate, see C. de Tischendorff, *Evangelia Apocrypha*, 2nd edn. (Leipzig, 1876), pp. 456–8; M. R. James, *Apocryphal New Testament* (1924), pp. 157–9. The story is in *SEL*, pp. 697–706.

LIV

f. 84ᵇ   HISTORIA JUDE ISCARIOT

f. 84ᵇ   [Legitur in quadam histo]ria quod quidam vir fuit [in Jerusalem, nomine Rube]n qui et alio nomine dictus est

.   .   .   .   .

f. 85ᵇ   in terra offenderat, [ab ang]elorum et hominum regione separaretur [et in a]yere cum demonibus sociaretur, etc.

There have been two important works on the medieval Life of Judas: P. F. Baum, 'The medieval legend of Judas Iscariot', *PMLA* xxxi (1916), 481–632; E. K. Rand, 'Medieval lives of Judas Iscariot' in *Anniversary Papers by Colleagues and Pupils of G. L. Kittredge* (Boston, 1913), pp. 305–16. For the relation of **T** to the versions discussed by Baum and Kittredge, see thesis, ii. 436–8. The most widely known version was that in the chapter 'De Sancto Mathia apostolo', *Legenda Aurea*, Ch. xlv, pp. 184–6.

A man named Ruben in Jerusalem had a wife Ciborea, who dreamed that she would give birth to a son who would destroy his race; when he was born she and her husband put him to sea in a basket, which drifted to the island of Scarioth (whence his surname); the childless queen of the island adopted him and passed him off as her own; when she had a legitimate son she began to ill-treat Judas, who soon learnt the truth about his birth, and killed the rightful heir. He fled to Jerusalem and entered the service of Pilate. One day Pilate sent Judas into an orchard to steal some apples; Judas was discovered by the owner, Ruben, and in the brawl killed Ruben, his own father. Pilate gave Judas all Ruben's property, including his wife

Ciborea. One night Ciborea lamented the events of her life, and Judas realized that he had committed patricide and incest. He joined Christ's disciples to earn forgiveness; when ointment was poured on Christ's feet instead of being sold for money which he would have stolen (*or*, of which he would have stolen the tenth part), as compensation he sold Christ for thirty denarii; in remorse he hanged himself, and 'his bowels gushed out', so that the lips which had kissed Christ would not be defiled; he is kept in the lower atmosphere by devils, having a place neither on earth nor in heaven.

The sources and later development of the Judas story are discussed in full by Baum; the *SEL* (pp. 692–7) probably used a separate life like this (one is found in Bodley MS. 90, where it follows a Life of Pilate), but the *Towneley Play*, xxxii ('*Suspencio Jude*'), may have used the *Legenda*.

LV

f. 85ᵇ   THE HOUSE OF WISDOM

f. 85ᵇ   Quod domus sapiencie dicitur claustrum: Domus
         sapiencie claustrum est, cuius [f]undamentum est
         paupertas, parietes obediencia et continencia, altitudo
         humilitas, tectum amor fraternitatis, septem columpne
         sunt septem obseruancie regulares, scilicet cibi aridi-
         tas, vestis asperitas, ieiuniorum continuacio, vigili-
         arum protraccio, manuum labor, discipline rigor;
         septima est oracionis instancia.

I have been unable to locate the source of this passage, and have seen no notice of it elsewhere. The most similar architectural allegory known to me is the interpretation of Prov. 9: 1 by Alanus ab Insulis, *Dicta mirabilia seu memorabilia* (*PL* ccx), pp. 261–2. Cf. also the *Benedictine Rule*, Ch. iv, end: 'Officina vero ubi haec omnia [praecepta] diligenter operemur, claustra sunt monasterii et stabilitas in congregatione.' See thesis, ii. 438–9.

LVI–LVII

f. 86ª   *ORACIO S[ANCTE VRITHE]*
               and COLLECT

> f. 86ª   Cotidiane lux di[ei]
>   Protulit ad laud[em] De[i]
>
> .   .   .   .   .
>
> O villa Chitelhamptonia
> Letare cum Deuonia
>   quod tal[iter se gesserit]
> Ora pro nobis virgo . . . per Cristum dominum nostrum.

Not in Walther. Not found elsewhere.

Ed. thesis, i. 192–3, ii. 439–41. See also M. R. James, 'St. Urith of Chittlehampton', *Proceedings of the Cambridge Antiquarian Soc.* x (1902), 230–4; James, *Catalogue*, iii. 502; J. F. Chanter, 'St. Urith of Chittlehampton: a study in an obscure Devon saint', *Trans. of the Devonshire Assoc.* xlvi (1914), 290–308—this leans heavily on James, without acknowledgement; J. H. B. Andrews, 'Chittlehampton', *Trans. Devonshire Assoc.* xciv (1962), 233–338 (partic. pp. 233–41, 333–5). The text is very badly damaged; my restorations are not always those of the printed texts.

St. Uritha is patron saint of Chittlehampton. This deficient poem is one of the few sources for her legend, which appears to be similar to that of St. Sidwell of Exeter: dedicated to Christ, she suffers martyrdom at the hands of scythers, who are acting on the orders of her stepmother; the scythers may have been swallowed up by the earth. A fountain springs up where the saint falls. The legend is probably pre-Saxon.

Metre: roughly that of a regular Victorine sequence: 2(8p), 7pp, 2(8p), 7pp, *aabccb*. Two of the five stanzas are very irregular, having more than the usual number of syllables in some lines.

APPENDIX I

TEXTS

(MAINLY ASSOCIATED WITH GLASTONBURY ABBEY)

I	Accounts: assessments of abbey lands
4	Feat of Gardeninge
X	Epitaphium D. Joseph
XVIII	Epiphany Hymn
XIX–XX	Hymn and Collect to the two St. Josephs
XXVI	'Ingratitudo' by Stephen Deverell, monk of Glastonbury
XLIX	'Conventual Diet' by Abbot Henry de Blois
L	Letter from Cologne (9 June 1434) from Abbot Nicholas Frome

All the above items are edited and annotated in full; only Nos. 4 and L have been printed previously. It should be noted that two other items in the MS. may owe their inclusion to associations with Glastonbury. No. XXVIII (Tryvytlam, 'De Laude Universitatis Oxonie', above, pp. 75–6), 269–364, contrasts the excellence of Glastonbury with the unruly behaviour of John Seen, one of its monks: opposite the first mention of the abbey,

> O quam Glastonia felix collegium!
> Vix habet Anglia tale cenobium.   (277–8),

the scribe has written what appears to be *nota* in the margin. The second part of No. XLVIII (St. Hilda) relates the flight of the monks of Whitby to Glastonbury with Hilda's relics:

> Suppressa patria fugiunt monachi palacia;
> Ipsos Glastonia recipit ductrice Maria.   (558–9).

Editorial practice follows that outlined above, p. 39. Abbreviations, which are standard, have been expanded without notice. In the English No. 4, all final flourishes have been ignored, except for a pronounced final curl sometimes found after *r*; þ has been expanded as *th* wherever a superscript letter or mark of suspension indicates that an abbreviation is intended; p with a stroke through the descender has been expanded as *per*, but in a few cases *par* was probably intended. Restorations, where the MS. is damaged, are in [. . .]; emendations are in ⟨. . .⟩; for the special use of these brackets, see below, p. 130.

I[1]

f. 1^b

[Summa] decime abbatis Glaston' in Somers'..........iiij li. xv s. vi.

[S]umma decime eiusdem in Wylts' et Barks'   xv li. iij s.

Summa decime eiusdem in Dors' et Sarum   xxiij li. viij s. j d.

Summa decime eiusdem in Deuonia   x s.

      Summa totalis   Cxxx li. xij s. ix d. ob.

      Inde medietas   lxv li. vj s. iiij d. ob.

Summa obedienciariorum de decima Glaston':

Decima Prioris	iiij s. viij d.
Sacriste	cxviij s.
Elemos'	c s. iij d. ob.
Camerar'	lxx s.
Precentor'	v s. v d.
..............r'	xxxviij s. iiij d.
.........iar'	xxix s. vij d. ob.
[In]firmar'	xij s. ij d.
Hostillar'	..... s.
Gardinar'	....
D[ecim]a soluenda d	viij s. viij d.
Summa totalis de .... totam baroniam Glaston'	
....	ij s. xi d. ob.
....	x li. xj s. v d. ob. q^a

This entry illustrates the original purpose of the book; it appears to be an assessment of Glastonbury property for the purpose of paying papal dues.

---

[1] No. 1. *This page is obscured by a large patch of damp.*

41

THE FEAT OF GARDENINGE

Ho so wyl a gardener be,
Here he may both hyre and se
Euery tyme of the ȝere and of the mone,
And how the crafte schall be done,
5 Yn what maner he schall delue and sette
Bothe yn drowthe and yn wette,
How he schall hys sedys sowe;
Of every moneth he most knowe,
Bothe of wortys and of leke,
10 Ownyns and of garleke,
Percely, clarey, and eke sage,
And all other herbage.

Off Settyng and Reryng of treys

Yn the calenders of Januare
Thu sc⟨hal⟩t treys both set and rere
15 To graffy theryn appyl and pere,
And what treys ys kynd hem to bere:
Appul and a appul tre,
For ther ys kynd ys most to be.
Of pere y mynde ȝorne
20 To graffe hym apon a hawthorne.

Of graffyng of treys

Thu myȝt graffe appul and pere
Fro the moneth of Septembre to Auerere.
Wyth a saw thu schalt the tre kytte
And wyth a knyfe smowth make hytte;
25 Kleue atweyne the stok of the tre
Whereyn that thy graffe schal be;

¹ No. 4. *Title by* **A** (*section headings by* **T**). 14 schalt: *MS.* sclatt.

Make thy kyttyng of thy graffe
Bytwyne the newe and the olde staffe,
So that hit be made to lyfe
30 As the bake and the egge of a knyfe;
A wegge thu sette yn myddys the tre,
That euery syde fro other fle,
Tyl hit be openyd wyde,
Whereyn the graffe schal be leyde.
35 The rynde of the graffe and the stok of the tre
Most acorde, how that hit ever be.
Also sone the graffe acordyth wyth the stok,
Take the wegge anone vp;
Vpon the stok all abowte
40 Clay mote be leyde to kepe the rayne owte:
For the schowrys of the rayne
Vpon the clay thu schalt mese layne.
f. 19ᵃ Wyth a wyth of hasel-tre rynde
The stoke fast thu bynde;
45 But thu do thys, y vnderstonde,
Al thy graff wul turne apon thy honde.
Yf he be graffyd at raysowne,
He wul bere the next saysowne.

    Of cuttyng and Settyng of Vynys

Of settyng of vynys we most haue yn mynde
50 How thay schal be sette al yn here kynde:
Whyle hit ys esterne wynde,
Thu schalt kytte nother sette no ⟨b⟩ynde;
When the wynde ys yn the west,
To kutte and to sette ys al ther best.
55 Yn thys maner thu schalt kytte the vynetre;
To be sette hit schal haue knottys þre:
Too schal be sette yn the grownde,
And one aboue for growynde.
Yn the lond where hyt schal growen ynne

52 bynde: *MS.* vynde.

60 Hyt wold aske to be dyȝte wyth dynge:
Euery ȝere wythouȝt drede
þey wold aske dyng abouȝt ham sprede.
Grow they wul sone and long be;
Than put vnder ham forkys of tre.
65 Of thys tale lete vs now stone
And to another we wul gone.

Of Settyng and Sowyng of Sedys

Yn the day of Seynt Valentyne
Thu schalt sowe this sedys yn tyme,
For they beþ herbys vnmeke;
70 Thu schalt ham set and sow eke.
They that bethe strong and nouȝt meke,
The names of hem ys garlek and leke.
Oynet thu schalt sow then,
Other therafter sone apon.
75 To set oynyns to make the sede
Y wul the tel for my mede:
Yn Auerell other yn Mars, as y haue yfownde,
To set other to sowe hem yn the grownde.
When they bygynnyth to growe hye,
80 Lete none of ham towche other nye.

f. 19ᵇ Vnder hem than put thu schall,
That none of hem downe nouȝt fall,
Yf thu wyl that hy the,
Forkys ymade of aschetre.
85 To haue ham saue and kepe hare prow
They wolde aske askys abowt ham ystrow.
When they rype, they wyl schow,
And by the bollys thu schalt hem know:
The sede wythyn wul schewe blake;
90 Then thu schalt hem vp take.
They wul be rype at the full
At Lammasse of Peter Apostull.
On thys maner thu schalt the sedys drye:

Vppon a clothe thu the sedys lye;
95 Aȝen the sonne his kynde ys
For to ly to dry ywys.
Hereof y can no more say,
But now y wul bygynne a new lay.

Of Sowyng and settyng of Wurtys

Wurtys we most haue
100 Bothe to mayster and to knaue;
Ye schul haue mynde here
To haue wurtys yong al tyme of the yere.
Euery moneth hath his name
To set and sow wythouȝt eny blame:
105 May for somer ys al the best,
July for eruyst ys the nexst,
Nouembre for wynter mote the thyrde be,
Mars for Lent, so mote y the.
The lond mote wel ydygnyd be,
110 Ydolue, ysturyd, syre, perde!
Whan thu hast ysow thi sede on long,
Foore wykys therafter thu let hem stonde;
Whan the iiij wykes beth al ouer gone,
Take thy plontys eueryone
115 And set ham yn kynd fat lond,
And thay wul fayre wurtys be and long;
Wythyn too wykes that they beth ysett
Thu may pul hem to thy mete.
And so fro moneth to monethe
120 Thu schalt bryng thy wurtys forthe.
f. 20ᵃ They that schal bere sede lasse and more,
Let ham grow to make the store.
Of wurtys can y no more telle;
Of other herbys hereafter y schelle.

Of the Kynde of Perselye

125 Further ouer passe y nell

Tyl y haue tolde the kynde of percell:
Percell kynde ys for to be
To be sow yn the monthe of Mars, so mote y the.
He wul grow long and thykke,
130 And euer as he growyth thu schalt hym kytte:
Thu may hym kytte by reson
þryes yn one seson,
Wurtys to make and sewes also.
Let hym neuer to hye go:
135 To lete hym grow to hye hit ys grete foly,
For he wul than blest and wanchy.
Hys kynde ys nouȝt to be sette—
To be sow ys al ther best.
Thay that the sede schal bere the,
140 Kytte hym nouȝt but lete hym be
Fro mydwynter to the Natyuyte,
And he schal fayre sede be.
Of percell ys lyȝt to know:
Take hede, he wul nouȝt be set but sow,
145 For yf he be set, he wul wax thynne,
And then he wul nouȝt be gode to rypyne.
Now hereof lete we be,
And to another we wul te.

Of other maner herbys

Of other herbys y schall telle,
150 Therfor y mote a stownd dwell.
Yn what moneth ys best ham sette and sow,
Sone hereafter thu schalt knowe:
Yn the moneth of Auerell
Set and sow ham euerydell;
155 Herbys to make bothe sawce and sewe,
Thu schalt haue ham here a-rewe.
Of al the herbys of Yrlonde,
Here thu schalt knowe meny onde:

148 *gap in MS. before* te (*presumably added later by* T).

Pelyter, dytawnder, rewe and sage,
160 Clarey, tyme, ysope and orage,
f. 20ᵇ Myntys, sauerey, tuncarse and spynage,
Letows, calamynte, auans and borage,
Fynel, sowthrynwode, warmot and rybwort,
Herbe Jon, herbe Robert, herbe Water and walwort,
165 Hertystonge, polypody, ⟨y⟩arrow and comfery,
Gromel, woderofe, hyndesall and betony,
Gladyn, valeryan, scabyas and spereworte,
Verueyn, wodesoure, waterlyly and lyuerworte,
Mouseere, egremoyne, honysoke and bugull.
170 Centory, horsel, adderstong and bygull,
Henbane, camemyl, wyldtesyl and stychewort,
Weybrede, growdyswyly, elysauwder and brysewort,
Merche, lauyndull, radysche, sanycle and seneuy,
Peruynke, violet, cowslyppe and lyly,
175 Carsyn, dyllys, strowberys and moderwort,
Langebefe, totesayne, tansay and feldewort,
Orpy, nepte, horehownd and flos campi,
Affodyll, redenay, primerole and oculus Cristi,
Rose ryde, rose why3te, foxgloue and pympernold,
180 Holyhocke, coryawnder, pyony and the wold.
All this herbys, by Seynt Mychaell,
Wold be sette yn the moneth of Auerell.
Further more wul y no3t go,
But here of herbys wul y ho.

      Of the kynde of Saferowne

185 Of saferowne we mote telle:
He schal be kepte fayre and welle.
Saferowne wul haue, wythou3t lesyng,
Beddys ymade wel wyth dyng.
For sothe yf thay schal bere,
190 Þay wold be sette yn the moneth of September
Three days byfore Seynt Mary day Natyuyte,

165 yarrow: *MS.* parrow. 175 carsyndyllys *as one word in MS.*

Other the next woke therafter, so mote y the.
Wyth a dybbyl thu schalt ham sette,
That the dybbyl byfore be blunt and grete;
195 Three ynchys depe they most sette be,
And thus seyde mayster Jon Gardener to me.

Explicit hic liber qui vocatur anglice Mayster Jon
Gardener.

Index and *Suppl.* 4146. Also in BM Addit. 20091 ff. 75ᵃ–78ᵃ (xix-c.
transcript of **T** by Thomas Wright); ibid. ff. 79ᵃ–80ᵇ (transcript by
Wright of a xiv-c. copy—not in the *Index* or *Suppl.*= **W**).

Ed. (from **T** only) thesis, i. 21–7, ii. 235–48; the Hon. Alicia
Amherst, 'A fifteenth century treatise on gardening', *Archaeologia*
liv (1894), 157–72. See also Amherst, *A History of Gardening in
England*, 3rd enlarged edn. (1910); Sir Frank Crisp, *Medieval
Gardens*, 2 vols. (1924), i. 43–4; W. L. Carter, in *My Garden* xxxvi
(Dec. 1936), 519–32. See also my article in *N. & Q.* ccxi (1966),
324–30, written without knowledge of Wright's transcript.

The Wright transcripts are in the first of five volumes which form
the 'Collections for a History of the Ballad Literature of Ireland by
Tho. Crofton Croker'; they are on small sheets of paper pasted into
the volume, and were presumably sent (some time between 1848 and
1854) to Croker by Wright, who may have thought the reference to
al the herbys of Yrlonde of interest to Croker. Croker annotated the
herbs in Wright's transcript of **T** on ff. 61–4 (he misread several of
the names).

The MS. from which Wright made his second transcript (**W**) is
unknown;[1] he prefaced it with the following remarks:

The following fragment of a rather earlier copy of the poem of John
the Gardener was copied from a manuscript in private hands, which
was in my possession for a few days. It was I think of the end of the
fourteenth century. There was I think a portion of the poem preceding
this, of which I have lost my transcript. This latter portion is curious
because it contains some concluding lines not in the Cambridge MS.

The fragment begins at line 157 of the **T** version, but the section on
the herbs is two lines shorter than that in **T**; it adds 31 lines after the
point at which the **T** version ends: these lines provide a conclusion to
the poem. The whole of the fragment is printed here:

193 dybbyl *above line, over* dyddyl *expunged.* 196 mas *crossed through before*
mayster.

[1] See Addendum on p.̣ 139.

157 Alle of the herbys o Ierlonde
Here thow schalt ham knowe eueri onde
Peletyr ditaw't'yr rew and sage
160 Clarey tyme yssope and orrage
161 Mintys sawery tuncarsse and spinage
Betus calament awas warmote and ribwort
164 Herb jone, herbe watere, herb Robert, and walwort
165 Hertistonge pollipody yarrow and conferi
Crommylle werwey hyndehale and bettony
Gladdyne waleryan violet and smerwort
Warmot wodsowre water lily and lywirwort
169 Mowshere egrimoyn honysoke and bugulle
171 Eskbam camemylle wildethesil and stichewort
Waybred lymyke ditany and brisswort
Merche lawandir raddys sankyl and horsselle
Growndesswily wotherstyl and lely
175 Carsyn straberriwisse modirwort and tansy
Halfewode fedwort horhownde and orpy
Wyolet redemay prymrolle attirlowberry
Finelle sowrynwod wetherwoth and carway
179 Rose red rose wyth holyhok and pempernolde
181 Alle thos herbys be seynt Michelle
Mot ben set in the monȝthe of averelle
Furthir can I noȝth go
But of herbys I wolle ho
185 But nedys I most mo telle
Of saffer how it schal be welle
 Saffer wolde have without lesyng
Beddis ymade well with dyng
Sothelich ȝyffe thay schal berre
190 Thay most ben set in the monȝthe of September
Thre days befor seynt Mari day Nativité
Ether the nexst wike ther affter, so mot I the
With a dibbil thow schalt ham sette
That the dibbil byfor be bothe blont and gret
195 Thre inchys dep thay most sette be
And so sayde maister John Gardener to me
*1 To gadir the safferyn I schal ȝow say
Fro Nativité to seynt Symonne and Jude is day
On what tyme of the day thow wolle
Thow myȝth hit bothe gadyr and pulle
*5 And so fro day to day
Tylle the tyme ben gone away
And affter Seynt Symonne and Jude is day
The kynde of blossum wolle gone away
And affter the v^{te} ȝere his ende other the ferthe
*10 Thow take up the safferyn of the herthe

And put ham in a chambire both clen and fayre
To hawe the kynde of the hey3ere
And atte the fest of Nativité
Put ham into the herthe a3ee
*15 And 3yf yow wolle haw gode safferyn
Let non wedis grow ham in
And so do fro 3ere to 3ere
As thy boke wolle the lere
This boke hath here y tolde
*20   Kepe this boke swy3e welle
I not non that suche tale can telle
Pray we to that holde gradener that is and ever was
That in hewen he grawnt hous a plas
To be in hys herbere that is so sweet
*25 That no synne fro thylke plas us lete
And that we mot oure synnis bette
Ar that we and de3t togadyr mete
To blis he us bryng a-ry3t
He may so welle,
*30 That he 3yf us part of hys ly3t,
Amen! so bedde we snelle

Explicit Garddener

In the list of herbs **W** names two plants twice (*violet* and *warmot*), includes nine which are not in **T** (*eskbam, lymyke, ditany, wotherstyll, halfewode, attirlowberry, wetherwoth, carway*, and *smerwort*), and omits the following twenty-three from **T**'s list: *borage, woderofe, scabyas, centory, adderstong, bygull, henbane, elysauwder, seneuy, peruynke, cowslyppe, dyllys, langebefe, totesayne, nepte, flos campi, affodyll, oculus Christi, foxgloue, spereworte, coryawnder, pyony*, and *wold*. *Betus* is an error (perhaps Wright's own) for *Letus*, and *awas* is for *awans*.

The omissions and the frequent failures of the rhyme scheme are probably sufficient evidence to dismiss the possibility that **W** was the original text of the poem, or even an early draft of it. Probably the original version of the herb section was a few lines longer than that preserved in **T**, with the herbs in substantially the same order; **W** has followed it closely in parts, but at times has garbled it considerably.

The problems of the origin of the poem are discussed in my article referred to above; the conclusions expressed there are only slightly affected by the discovery of Wright's transcript of **W**. Amherst and dependent authorities were impressed by the absence from the poem of any reference to exotic plants or any instructions which implied a warm climate, features which are derived from Classical treatises and which disfigure much Middle English gardening literature; they therefore suggested that the poem was an original treatise composed by someone with a practical knowledge of gardening. There are several reasons for disputing this inference. Despite the brevity of the poem, it is divided somewhat pretentiously into sections with headings, some of which describe the contents accurately, others less so—lines 13–20, for instance, deal only with the grafting of trees, not their 'rearing'; lines 67–98 mention only the sowing of hardy plants (and that very briefly), and then go on to deal exclusively with the limited topic of growing onions for seed. The promise in 5–6, that the prospective gardener will learn how to dig and plant in wet and dry weather, is never fulfilled. The herb list (in **T**) includes for April sowing such unlikely plants as waterlily and the moss liverwort. The passage which describes the sowing of *wurtys* (111–18) implies that it is possible to grow cabbages from seed to maturity in six weeks, a 'feat' impossible even with the quick-growing lettuce. The selection of topics can readily be seen to be very haphazard, and several very minor matters are given a wholly disproportionate amount of space. These points, taken together with the reference in the colophon to the poem as a *liber* (cf. **W** *18–*20) and perhaps the implication that there was a title other than the English one, lead one to suppose that the poem was an abridgement of a much longer work, perhaps a Latin treatise in prose. In my article there is an account of the development and handling in Middle English of Palladius's *De Re Rustica*, which was translated, annotated, rewritten, and abridged: extracts were made from the newly 'edited' version and circulated separately. I would suggest that the 'Feat of Gardeninge' may be the result of a similar process.

The name 'Jon Gardener' is almost certainly a literary fiction; Amherst noted someone of this name as the beneficiary of the will of Nicholas Sturgeon, a priest buried in St. Paul's, who left money to St. Augustine's, Canterbury, and to churches in the west of England (*Fifty Earliest English Wills*, ed. F. J. Furnivall, EETS, 78 (1882), p. 133). Amherst localized the poem in the south-east or London area, partly because of the fame at the time of the gardens and orchards of Kent, and partly because of Skeat's (private) opinion that the language of the poem was Kentish; neither argument has any validity.

The language of the poem is markedly different from that of the other English items in the MS. Weakening of final /ŋg/ and /nd/ is indicated by several rhymes (59–60, 65–6, 111–12, 115–16, 157–8). This poem has only *h*-forms of the oblique cases of the 3rd plural pronoun (see above, pp. 15–16), and *hy* (83) is the only *h*-form of the nominative in the MS. The *y*- prefix in the pt. pp. is more common in this poem, as is the infinitive suffix *-n* (*-en, -yn*). The distinct plural form *schul* (101) is not found elsewhere, and the dialectal *schelle* (124, confirmed by rhyme) is also unique to this poem. Many dialectal variants seem to have employed for the sake of the rhyme, e.g. *wyde*: *leyde* (33–4: see p. 13). For further details, see thesis, ii. 238–9.

Several of the couplets employ assonance rather than rhyme, and sometimes scarcely even that (cf. 37–8, 73–4, 119–20, 129–30, etc.). Some of the lines can be scanned as octosyllabic couplets, but the majority will not fit any normal pattern of scansion, even as four-stressed 'broken-backed' lines.

13–18. 'At the beginning of January you must set and rear trees on which to graft apple and pear and whatever trees it is natural for them to bear: for instance, apple and an apple-tree, for there (in an apple-tree) its (the apple's) nature is most appropriate to be (implanted)'; or, if *treys* (16) is the object of *set and rere*, '. . . you must set and rear trees on which to graft apple and pear, and (plant) whatever trees naturally bear them (apple and pear). . . .' In either case, *treys* (14) seems to refer to service-trees, which were thought to be particularly suitable to receive graftings, partly because of false etymology of OE *syrfe* (as though it were *serve*).

13. *calenders* (confused with *Calends*): the only example in this sense, but see *MED calender* 4a–4c.

22. *Auerere* (adapted for the rhyme): this form is not recorded elsewhere.

23–48. *tre* (23) refers to the new graft, which must be cut with a saw and made smooth with a knife; a cleavage should be made in the stock into which the graft is to be placed. 27–30 appears to mean that the cross-section of the grafting should look like that of a knife, i.e. wedge-shaped, like the section of a single-edged chef's knife. The various methods of grafting are described in detail in the Middle English *Palladius on Husbondrie* iii. 50–61, ed. B. Lodge, EETS 52, 72 (1872–9), and the phraseology is very similar to that used here.

46. *turne apon thy honde* 'turn out unsuccessful for you': not in *OED*. Perhaps a special sense of *turn* 'go bad'.

52–4. *kytte, kutte*, appear to refer to making cuttings for transplanting rather than to pruning.

55. *Yn thys maner*: unless this refers forward to cutting the shoot in such a way that there are three knots, a few lines must be missing.

68. *this*: *thi* would be a better reading.

73. *oynet*: not in *OED* with *-et* suffix (OF *oignonet*), but see also Balliol MS. 354, f. 110[b].

88. *bollys*: the seed-vessels.

92. 1 August.

99. *wurtys*: probably cabbage. For the implications of the notion that they can be grown to maturity in six weeks, see above.

133. *wurtys*: here 'pottage' (*OED* sb.[1], 3, pl.).

136. *wanchy* 'wither': for the form, cp. *OED vanish*.

141. The Nativity of the Virgin, 8 September.

159–80. This list may well have been derived directly from a herbal: it includes such inappropriate plants as waterlily, the moss liverwort, and the fern adder's-tongue, none of which is likely to be sown in April. The following notes deal only with those herbs whose identities are not self-evident and undisputed, except for a few which are of interest for other reasons. Reference is made to: *Agnus Castus*: *a Middle English Herbal*, ed. G. Brodin (Uppsala, 1950) (AC); *A Middle English Translation of Macer Floridus 'De Viribus Herbarum'*, ed. G. Frisk (Uppsala, 1949) (Macer); J. Earle, *English Plant Names from the Tenth to the Fifteenth Century* (1880); R. C. A. Prior, *Popular Names of British Plants*, 3rd edn. (1879); J. Britten and R. Holland, *Dictionary of English Plant Names* (English Dialect Society, xxii, xxvi, xlv, 1878–84).

pelyter: probably Pellitory-of-Spain, *Anacyclus pyrethrum* (AC 214, Macer 37a10) rather than Amherst's Pellitory-of-the-wall, *Parietaria officinalis* (*OED* 1548–) recorded only with *-y*, *-ie*, endings.

dytawnder: probably Broad-leaved pepperwort, *Lepidium latifolium*. Also possible is Dittany-of-Crete (listed separately in W); for the confusion between the two, see AC 181. 7 (ante-dating *OED* 1548).

orage: Orach, *Atriplex hortensis* (Macer 21a20, Prior, pp. 171–2); the the suffix shows unstressed /tʃ/ > /dʒ/, also influenced by *borage*, etc.

tuncarse: town-cress, *Lepidium sativum*.

spynage: Spinach (*OED* 1530, AC 156.12, *c.* 1400): for the suffix, cf. *orage*.

warmot: Wormwood, *Artemisia abrotanum* (this form in *OED* only −1450).

herbe Jon: St. John's wort, *Hypericum perforatum* (AC 192.7).

herbe Water: Herb Walter (not in *OED*: see AC 191.9 *note* for further references). It sometimes means woodruff (which is in 166) and lily-of-the-valley (but this does not fit the description in AC). For a full discussion, see thesis, ii. 245.

walwort: (*a*) Danewort, Dwarf elder, *Sambucus ebulus* (Prior, p. 247, Earle, pp. 13, 43); (*b*) Wall-pepper, *Sedum acre*. For other identifications, less likely here, see Britten and Holland, p. 483.

gromel: Gromwell, *Lithospermum officinale*.

woderofe: Woodruff, *Asperula odorata*.

hyndesall: Hindheal, Wood sage, *Teucrum scorodonia* (*OED*, Earle, pp. 37, 43). Not found elsewhere with medial *s* (by analogy with *hertystonge*, etc.).

sperewort: Buttercup, *Ranunculus lingua*. Earlier usages include Elecampane (–1265) and Nep (–1000).

wodesoure: Wood sorrel, *Oxalis acetosella*.

waterlyly: Water lily, *Nymphaea alba* (*OED* 1549–, but cf. Earle, p. 49, AC 216.3).

lyuerworte: the moss Liverwort, *Marchantia polymorpha* (AC 185.12, despite Brodin's note).

mouseere: (*a*) Hawkweed, *Hieracium pilosella* (so AC 166.30), (*b*) Chickweed, *Cerastium vulgatum*.

egremoyne: Agrimony, *Agrimonia eupatoria*.

honysoke: uncertain. Early glosses (Earle, pp. 19, 30) give it as *ligustrum*, cowslip or primrose; somewhat later (Earle, p. 46) it appears to refer to meadow clover. The first certain example in the PrE sense, Woodbine, *Lonicera periclymenus*, is for 1548 (*OED*).

horsel: Horse-heal, elecampane, *Inula helenium*.

adderstong: the fern Adder's-tongue, *Ophioglossum vulgatum* (*OED* 1578; five other senses in Britten and Holland, p. 6).

bygull: perhaps corrupt—there is no equivalent in W. Amherst, followed by *MED*, interprets as Bigold, corn marigold, *Chrysanthemum segetum*. Croker misread Wright's transcript as *byȝull* which he interpreted as 'basil': this is unlikely. Thesis, ii. 246–7, suggests *pygull* (*OED pigle*); however, this normally = Stichwort (which is in the next line), and confusion with *paigle*, cowslip, was not made until later: see Skeat, *N. & Q.* 6th ser., vii (1883), 405, 455, Prior, p. 175.

growndyswyly: Groundsel, *Senecio vulgaris*.

elysauwder: Alexanders, *Smyrnium olusatrum* (no forms with initial *e* in *OED* or *MED*); for the omission of medial *n*, see above, p. 14.

brysewort: Bruisewort, daisy, *Bellis perennis*.

merche: March, a kind of celery, *Apium* (*graveolus*).

lauyndull: Lavender, *Lavandula officinalis* (no form with an *l*-suffix in *OED*: it is derived directly from Medieval Latin *lavendula*).

seneuy: Mustard, *Brassica alba* (or *nigra*). It would be possible to read *seueny*, Savin, *Juniperus sabina* (although *OED* only records *sav*-forms). Amherst inconsistently reads *seueny* but glosses *Brassica*.

carsyn: Cresses, presumably *Nasturtium officinale* (for town-cress, *Lepidium sativum*, see above). The form with final *-yn* is not recorded elsewhere, but is confirmed in this poem by **W**.

dyllys: ? kinds of dill, *Anetum graveolens*; Amherst's suggestion, 'lilies', is unlikely: *lyly* is in 174.

strowberys: Strawberries (no form with *strow-* in *OED*, but cf. *straw* sb.¹).

moderwort: Mugwort, *Artemisia vulgaris* (Macer lal, Prior, p. 161).

langebefe: (*a*) Oxtongue, *Picris echoides*, (*b*) Bugloss. *OED langue de boeuf* records only forms with a medial *d(e)*.

totesayne: Tutsan, *Hypericum androsaemum*.

feldewort: Felwort, *Gentiana lutea*, also called Baldmoney until the Sixteenth Century (AC 189.27).

orpy: Orpine, *Sedum telephium* (Prior, p. 173). Not found elsewhere without final *-n* (but confirmed for this poem by **W** in rhyme).

nepte: Catmint, *Nepeta cataria* (AC 209.26, Prior, p. 166, Britten and Holland, p. 353); there is no need for Amherst's '. . . or turnip'.

flos campi: probably the Campion, *Lychnis* (so Amherst and *MED*). AC 182.5 says that *Daucus creticus* is sometimes called *flos campe* [*sic*], but its description of *Daucus* (normally the carrot) is like neither the carrot nor the campion.

redenay: unknown. Amherst glosses 'Red Ray, *Lollium perenne*' (*OED* 1578–, Prior, p. 196), but does not emend her text. **W** (173) has *redemay* which is equally difficult.

oculus Cristi: Wild clary, *Salvia verbenaca*.

pympernold: (*a*) Great Burnet, *Sanguisorba officinalis*, (*b*) Scarlet Pimpernel, *Anagallis arvensis* (xv c. in *OED*). *OED* records several *-nol* endings, but no forms with final *-d* (confirmed by W *pempernolde*).

holyhocke: some kind of Mallow, *Malva*: the common garden holly-hock (*Althea*) is a later importation.

wold: weld, *Reseda luteola*.

XI[1]

f. 28[b]   EPITAPHIUM D. JOSEPH

Hic iacet ⟨excultus⟩ Joseph pater ille sepultus,
Qui Cristum sciuit ac defunctum sepeliuit;
Hanc dedit iste domum matri Cristi fabricari,
Post Eue pomum qua posset homo reparari;
5 Pro nobis igitur oret noster pater iste
Per quem dirigitur tibi laus et honor, pie Criste. Amen.

Not in Walther. It is not strictly an epitaph: *hic iacet* means 'here [in Glastonbury] lies'. The monks of Glastonbury on the whole believed that Joseph of Arimathea was buried there: John of Glastonbury mentions the site of the tomb near a 'line' dividing the chapels of the Lady Chapel (at the east end of the presbytery), 'iuxta quam lineam, secundum quosdam antiquorum, jacet Sanctus Joseph' (John of Glastonbury, i. 2–3, 30, 54–6: one of the authorities was the poet Melkinus). In 1345 a royal writ was issued to one John Blome, giving him permission to search for the tomb; an East Anglian chronicle mentions that in 1367 the bodies of Joseph and his companions were found in the abbey. Both of these events are ignored by John of Glastonbury, and it seems improbable that in the fifteenth century the discovery of Joseph's tomb would have escaped wider notice. For the same reason we may doubt the authenticity of this 'epitaph', which has never previously been noticed.

See Joseph Armitage Robinson, *Two Glastonbury Legends* (1926), pp. 60–5. A life *De Sancto Joseph de Armathia* is included in *NLA* ii. 78–82; according to Horstman, it is based on John of Glastonbury's account, somewhat abbreviated.

Metre: mixed Leonine hexameters.

XVIII[2]

f. 44[a]   EPIPHANY HYMN

1. Gaudent in Epiphania
    Jesus, Joseph et Maria,
    magorum muneribus;

[1] No. X. *Title by* **A.** 1 excultus *by hand* **A** *above* sepultus *crossed through.*
[2] No. XVIII. *No title in MS.*

Omnes ergo gaudeamus,
Et hiis tribus offeramus
    corda, preces, laudibus:

2. Salue, puer, nuper nate,
Et pro tua pietate
    salua nos a crimine;
Salue, circumcise Jesu
Nosque tuo sana Iesu
    pro Maria virgine.

3. Aue, virgo, mater, prole,
Stella maris, celi sole,
    ad quos stella venerat:
Tribus magis hec illuxit
Et in Bethlem hos perduxit
    supra vosque manserat.

4. Tunc intrantes stella duce
Et gauisi noua luce
    adorabant Dominum,
Offerentes hunc thesaurum
Cristo—mirram, thus et aurum
    Saluatori hominum.

5. Gaude, Joseph cum Maria,
Qui magorum digna tria
    suscepistis munera:
Aurum regi eternali,
Et thus Deo, sed mortali,
    mirram propter funera.

6. Vale, Jesu, rex cunctorum,
Vere Deus seculorum,
Pro peccatis miserorum
    qui mortalis fueras;

3/6 manserat *above* stabat *expunged.*

Sed quia resurrexisti
Et ad celos ascendisti,
Cunctis nobis quos fecisti
    regnum tuum conferas.

7. Vale, virgo, mater Dei,
    Offerendo preces ei,
    Pietate memor mei
    Peccatoris valde rei
        viciorum macula;
    Vale, Joseph, orans secum,
    Vt sit Jesus semper mecum,
    Et vestrarum ope precum
    Valeamus omnes tecum
        per eterna secula.
        Amen

Not in Walther or Chevalier (under 1/1 or 5/1).

Ed. thesis, i. 97–9, ii. 310–11; otherwise unprinted and unnoticed.

James, *Catalogue*, lists stanzas 1–4 and 5–7 as two separate poems, and in the MS. 1–4 are written as verse, but 5–7 as prose. The following lines begin with a rubric initial: 5/1, 6/1, 7/1, 7/6; there are red marks through the initial letters of the following lines: 5/4–6, 6/2–3, 6/5, 6/7, 7/7–9, and *Amen*. The second part of this hymn is thus the most elaborately 'decorated' piece in the MS. However, there is no reason to split the hymn in two: the sense is continuous, and there is no prayer or *Amen* after 4/6. Moreover, the rhyme scheme argues for the unity of the hymn: the metre is that of the *Stabat mater dolorosa*, the regular sequence, and the rhyme scheme 1–4 *aabccb*, 5 *aabccb*, 6 *aaabcccb*, 7 *aaaabccccb*. This parallels exactly the sequence by Adam of St. Victor on 'The Nativity of the Virgin' (*OBMLV*, No. 163, pp. 232–4), in which the first eight stanzas rhyme *aabccb*, followed by four stanzas *abab*, and the last three stanzas increase in length as here. Other examples include *OBMLV*, Nos. 147, 164, etc.

Nothing can be said about the author or date: the hymn is an accomplished regular sequence in the Victorine manner, and could well be the work of the Glastonbury monk who wrote No. XIX below.

2/5. *Iesu* = *læsura*, the wound of circumcision; not found elsewhere.

3/1–2. *prole . . . celi sole*: 'because of your son, the sun of the sky.'

5/4–6. The symbolism is standard: cf. Prudentius, *Cathemerinon* xii (Epiphany), 69–72; *AH* liii, Nos. 28, 30, liv, Nos. 3, 4, and 105. The early commentators interpreted the gifts in the same, or similar, ways: Cassiodorus (*PL* lxx. 1060, on Cant. 1 : 12 and Matt. 27: 59); Raban Maur (*PL* cxii. 869–70, 999, 1070); Alcuin (*PL* c, 1114, on Apoc. 3: 18); *Glossa Ordinaria*, in *Biblia Sacra cum Glossa Ordinaria*, 6 vols. (Lyons, 1590), v. 62–3, on Matt. 2: 11.

7/3–5. '(Be) mindful of me, a sinner, truly guilty because of the stain of sins.'

XIX–XX[1]

f. 44b   HYMN AND COLLECT TO THE
                         ST. JOSEPHS

f. 44ᵇ   1.   Salue, pater, qui fuisti
                  Desponsatus matri Cristi
                  Et hunc natum qui vidisti,
                           Sancte Joseph senior;
                  Salue, pater, qui petisti
                  A Pilato corpus Cristi,
                  Quod de cruce suscepisti,
                           Sancte Joseph iunior.

         2.   Aue, senior, quem pastores
                  Inuenerunt iuxta flores
                  Bethlemites dulciores
                           Matrem atque filium.
                  Aue, iunior, qui vngebas
                  Corpus Jesu, quod tradebas
                  Sepulture quam habebas
                           Matris per auxilium.

Nos. XIX–XX. *No titles in MS.*

3. Gaude, senior, qui per stellam
   Magos Cristum et puellam
   Sponsam tuam tam tenellam
       Adorare videras;
   Gaude, iunior, post sepultum
   Jesum quem amabas multum
   Resurgentis videns vultum
       Pridie quem planxeras.

4. Euge, senior, vi sermonis
   Obstupescens Symeonis
   Sponse tue passionis
       Prophetantis gladium;
   Euge, iunior, qui seruasti
   Cristi matrem quam amasti,
   Et hic tandem predicasti
       Vtriusque gaudium.

5. Vale, senior, qui quesisti
   Cum Maria, corde tristi,
   Jesum quem post inuenisti
       Templo cum doctoribus;
   Vale, iunior, querens Angliam,
   Qui intrasti tunc Glastoniam
   Et fundasti hic ecclesiam
       Primam in hiis partibus.

6. Senior, iunior, congaudete;
   In memoria nos tenete,
   Et in Domino iam valete,
       Joseph, Joseph, pariter,
   Quem pro nobis, supplicamus,
   Exoretis dum hic stamus,
   Vt post mortem valeamus
       Viuere perhenniter.

Sancte Joseph bine, iam cum Cristo sine fine,
Quesumus, orate pro nobis ex pietate:
Domine Jesu Criste, qui gloriosissimam virginem, matrem
tuam, beato Joseph seniori diuino consilio desponsare
volueras, et alterum Joseph decurionem, patronum no-
strum, de cruce te deponere ac sepelire permiseras, concede
nobis propicius, vt meritis amborum ac precibus, quorum
preconiis deuocius alternatim recolimus, et resurreccionis
tue gloria et desponsacionis perpetue copula gaudeamus.
Per te, Jesu Criste, qui cum Deo patre et Spiritu Sancto
viuit et regnat Deus. Amen.

Not in Walther or Chevalier. Although the cult of Joseph of Nazareth
was a late-medieval one, this cannot be used to establish the date of
this poem: the local associations of Joseph of Arimathea may have
contributed to an earlier literature on his namesake as well. Two
other poems to the elder Joseph are in *AH* liv. No. 50, and lv.
No. 197; on the latter, Blume notes that the appearance of the Joseph
cult so late in the Middle Ages resulted in a deficiency of hymns
to him which the humanists were unable to remedy.

Metre: regular Victorine sequence, 3(8p), 7pp, 3(8p), 7pp. In 5/5–7
each line has nine syllables, unless the *i* in *Angliam*, etc., is semi-
consonantal. In 6/3 *Domino* may be disyllabic (*Domno*).

XIX: 3/6 *Jesum*: perhaps read *Jesu*, gen. sg.

4/1–4 'Rejoice, elder, standing amazed at the force of the speech of
Simeon prophesying the sword of the Passion of your bride'
(Luc. 2: 34–5).

4/5 *seruasti* 'protected' or 'kept (in memory)' or 'served'—*seruare* in
ML often has the sense of *seruire* (*RWL*).

4/7–8, 'here in Glastonbury you finally preached the Joy of the Son
and Mother.'

XX: *quorum . . . recolimus*: *recolo* 'reflect upon' takes the gen. in
ML (*RWL*).

XXVI[1]

INGRATITUDO

Voluenti plurima in cordis speculo
Ingratitudinis occurrit racio,
Que mentem vulnerat dolore nimio
Et vultum inficit colore liuido.

5 In vultu cernitur color cinereus,
Membra contremulant tocius corporis,
Furtiue lacrimas effundit oculus
Facta recogitans ingratitudinis.

Quis scribe calamus scribentis propere,
10 Que vox, que poterit linguaue dicere,
Que mentis racio scit comprehendere
Quot mala veniunt ingratitudine?

Num primus angelus ingratitudine
Equari Domino similitudine
15 Si posset voluit? Ob hoc iustissime
E celo corruit suo pro scelere.

Sic Adam genitor humani sobolis
Gustando vetitum fit nocens plurimis;
Confossus vulnere ingratitudinis
20 Equari voluit diuinis sensibus.

In Genesi legitur quarto capitulo
Electi sanguinis Abel effusio.
Cur? Quia Domino in sacrificio
Placet, perimitur ingrati gladio.

[1] No. XXVI. *Title by* **D.**

25 Rex quidem Gerare ingratus fuerat,
    Qui iustum Ysaac cum suis spreuerat,
    Jurgans pro puteis quos nunquam foderat,
    Qui cuncta sufferens Bethel tetenderat.

    Ingratitudinis O mala gracia!
30 Joseph Egypciis vendens fallacia
    Lusisti Israel rubrata tunica
    Dicens, 'Tu filii vestem considera!'

    Ingrati murmurant en contra Dominum;
    Hebrey Moysen iurgant mitissimum;
35 Manna fastidiunt cibum dulcissimum
    Optantes regredi ad ollas carnium.

    Sic, sic, Abymelec, tu fratres perimis
    Transfossus iaculo ingratitudinis.
    Ingrata Dalida Sampsonem viribus
40 Euacuauerat abscisis crinibus.

    Nabot Carmelus fit Dauid nunci⟨i⟩s
    Ingratus nimium verbis pacificis:
    Spectis Abigayl vxoris precibus
    Sic stultus moritur suis stulticiis.

45 Abner et Amasa testantur siquidem
    Ducis milicie ingratitudinem;
    Ingratus Semey Dauid penuriem
    Irrisit lapides spargens et puluerem.

    Ingratus nimium Saul fortis robore
50 Dauid gratissimum nitens transfodere
    Parcendo Amalec quam debes perdere,
    Regno deiceris Agag pro scelere.

f. 48ᵃ   Decorus Absalon multum amabilis
         Traiectus lancea ingratitudinis
55   Vilis efficitur et despicabilis
         In quercu pendulus transfossus lanceis.

41 nunciis: *MS.* nuncius.

Achab et Jesabel Nabot diligerent,
Prophetas Domini in pace sinerent,
Et Joram sanguinem canes non lingerent,
60 In campo Ysrael si grati fierent.

Ingrati siquidem Anania⟨s⟩, Saphira,
Qui sancti spiritus abusi gracia
Petro discipulis dantes mendacia,
De rebus venditis retin⟨ent⟩ precia.

65 O Nero, traditor Dei et hominis,
O malus omnibus, O tibi pessimus,
Ingratitudinem tuam dant verius
Vrbs, mater, Seneca, Petrus apostolus.

Ad quid vlterius moror? Nunc breuiter
70 Audi sequentibus, credeque firmiter:
Ingratitudine dico veraciter
Nunquam eueniet quicquam feliciter.

Ingratum reprobant tot testimonia,
Non solum scribere verum interea
75 Pudet et dicere tibi propterea.
Ve quisquis talis es! Sit nunc inantea.

Ingratum dampnant Cristus et omnia,
Lex et natura cuncta per secula.
Jura tristantur huius natalia,
80 Quod vmquam fuerit in spera terrea.

Bonum ingratus cum operabitur,
Lupus per agnum tunc effugabitur;
Cor Pharaonis mel estimabitur;
Egeas siquidem pena priuabitur.

85 Suos dampnatos Auernus euomet;
Liuens Olibrius agnus deueniet,
Et Babel sydera turris pertransiet;
Auarum fuluor auri tunc saciet.

61 Ananias: *MS* Anania. 64 retinent: *MS.* retinentes.

Abel oblacio cum displicuerat,
90 Primas pugnancium et petras spreuerat,
Petrus fiducie petram et fregerat:
Ingratus siquidem tunc benefecerat.

Noe diluui⟨o⟩ dimersu⟨s⟩ fuerat;
Ignis Laurencium et reprobauerat;
95 Susanne vicio cor et viluerat,
Ingratus veritas quando dilexerat.

Lugentis lacrime tracte suspirio
Restringunt calamum vt a proposito
Desistam; carminis sit hec conclusio:
100 Valete grati semper in Domino. Amen.

Explicit tractatus de ingratitudine editus a Fratre
Stephano Deuerell, monacho Glastoniensi.

Walther 20794; otherwise unnoticed. In the colophon *editus* could
mean simply 'copied out', but it probably means that Stephen
adapted and produced the poem, perhaps from a prose original: this
is certainly not a holograph—there are errors at 41, 64, and 93.
Stephen's name is not found in any of the lists of Glastonbury
monks (see above pp. 9–10).

The poem is a simple complaint against ingratitude; it draws on
exempla mainly of Biblical origin, which may have been found
assembled together in a single tract. Many of the examples, but by
no means all, are found in Boccaccio's *De casibus illustrium virorum*
(facsimile of the Paris edn. of 1520, with an Introduction by L. B.
Hall, Gainesville, Fa., 1962): this includes the account of Nero's
slaying of Peter, but this was a common medieval legend. The spelling *Dalida* (39) gives no indication of the source (see note). The
theme of the poem recalls some passages from the poems dealing with
the friars (xxix and xxxi), but there is no suggestion that the poem
was written with a particular group of people in mind.

Metre: rhythmical asclepiads in four-line stanzas; first half-line with
five syllables (a licence I have seen frequently used, but not recorded
by Norberg) at 41, 79, 81–3, 85, 88. First half-line with extra unstressed syllable (also found elsewhere) at 21.

93 diluuio dimersus: *MS.* diluuium dimersum.

25-8. Gen. 26, 28. The syntax suggests that the antecedent of *qui* 28 is *Ysaac*, but it was in fact Jacob who founded the camp at Bethel (Gen. 28: 18-19). The subject of *foderat* is *rex Gerare*, Abimelech.

29-32. Gen. 37. Translate: 'O evil-favoured Ingratitude! By selling Joseph to the Egyptians with a trick, you deceived Israel (i.e. Jacob, Gen. 32: 28) by the cloak reddened with blood, saying "Behold the robe of your son!".'

33-6. Num. 11: 1-9; the phrase *ollas carnium* is from Exod. 16: 3.

37-8. Judic. 9: 1-5; this is Abimelech, son of Jerobaal, not the King of Gerar of Gen. 26 (above, 25-8).

39-40. Judic. 16. The spelling *Dalida* (Vulgate usually *Dalila*) is discussed with reference to Chaucer *CT MkT*, VII. 2063, and *BD* 738, by G. W. Landrum, 'Chaucer's use of the Vulgate', *PMLA* xxxix (1924), 75-100 (partic. p. 89). She records examples in the *Roman de la Rose*, the *Speculum Historiale*, *Cursor Mundi*, *Confessio Amantis*, and Deguileville's *Pilgrimage of the Life of Man*. To these may be added Lydgate *FP* i. 6414, etc. (but not the original Boccaccio, sig. B5^r, ed. cit. p. 45) and *Carm. Bur.* 23. 3/7 (see Hilka-Schumann, II, 37 for further cases). The probable source of the spelling is the Septuagint (Judic. 16: 4, etc.) where some MSS. have Δαλιδα for Δαλιλα; the form with *d* is also found in some MSS. of the Vulgate.

41-4. 1 Reg. 25. Translate: 'Nabot the Carmelite was ungrateful to the messengers of David [and] to their peaceful words; when he considered the prayers of his wife Abigail he died, foolish with all his follies.' The emendation *nunciis* is necessitated by the story, but I have left *Nabot* (Vulgate *Nabal*) as the poet may genuinely have confused Nabal with the Nabot of 3 Reg. 21.

43-4. 1 Reg. 25: 7.

44. cf. 1 Reg. 25: 25.

45-6. *ducis*: Joab, who killed Abner and Amasa (2 Reg. 3: 26-7 and 20: 8-13), both of whom were loved and bitterly lamented by David (cf. 3 Reg. 2: 32).

47-8. 2 Reg. 16: 5-13; the subject is *Semey*.

49-52. Apostrophe to Saul: 'You also [are] exceedingly ungrateful, Saul, strong in body, in attempting to slay . . . David: by sparing the city of Amalec which you ought to destroy you will be cast down from your throne because of the crime of Agag.' For Saul's first hatred of David, see 1 Reg. 18: 8-11, 19: 9-10; his disobedient failure to sack Amalec and his sparing of Agag and the best property are described in 1 Reg. 15; God's anger and vengeance are revealed in 1 Reg. 15: 23.

53–6. For the killing of Absalon by Joab see 2 Reg. 18; line 52 must mean that Absalon was pierced by the spear of Joab's ingratitude: this is in contrast with the image of 38.

57. *Nabot*: 3 Reg. 21; cf. above on 41–4.

58. The *prophetae Domini* killed by Jezabel: 3 Reg. 18: 4, 13.

59. There seems to be some confusion here: the death of Joram is recorded in 4 Reg. 9: 24, but his body is not licked by the dogs in the field. This fate is prophesied for Achab, father of Joram, by Elias (see 3 Reg. 21: 19); the prophecy is fulfilled in 3 Reg. 22: 38. The confusion may have been caused by 4 Reg. 9: 36: 'in agro Jezrahel comedent canes carnes Jezabel.'

61–4. Act. 5: 1–11: Ananias and Saphira withheld from the apostles the profit made from the sale of their lands. MS. *Anania* could be vocative, but *retinentes*, although corrupt, cannot be for *retinetis*, for metrical reasons. The second half of 61 must be read with an extra unstressed syllable (found elsewhere, but not common): the stanza may still be corrupt.

65–8. Peter's death in the Neronian persecution of A.D. 64–8 may well be a historical fact, and was certainly believed in the Middle Ages: cf. Lydgate *FP* vii, 749–50 (translating Boccaccio, *De Casibus*, sig. N5ᵛ, ed. cit., p. 178).

76. *sit nunc inantea*: 'let us now proceed' (cf. DC *inante(a)* 'in posterum') or 'enough of that, let that pass' (cf. *RWL* 'beforehand').

81–96. For the topos of the 'World upside-down', see E. R. Curtius, *European Literature and the Latin Middle Ages*, transl. W. R. Trask, Bollingen Ser. xxxvi (New York, 1952), p. 94 ff. Several of the *adynata* are perplexing: the list seems to be the poet's own.

82. Cf. Virgil, *Ecloga*, viii. 53.

83. Exod. 7: 3, 13, etc.

84. *Egeas*: i.e. Aegeus. This is probably not the Athenian Aegeus, father of Theseus: as a pagan he would naturally be in hell, but there seems no reason why he should have been singled out for mention. More likely is the proconsul Aegeus who was responsible for the martyrdom of St. Andrew the Apostle. The story was known from the *Legenda Aurea*, among other sources.

86. 'Angry Olibrius will turn out to be a lamb'. The prefect Olybrius was the suitor and persecutor of St. Margaret: the account of her martyrdom is included in many works, the *Legenda Aurea*, Bokenham's *Legendys of Hooly Wummen*, Lydgate *MP* i, 137–92. For an account of the tradition, see F. M. Mack, *Seinte Marherete*, EETS 193 (1934), pp. ix–xii.

90. Of the several possible interpretations, the most likely seems to be: 'the leader of the warriors [Goliath] despised the stones [thrown by David]'—i.e. Goliath was not killed: it is unlikely that David himself should be called a *primas pugnancium* at this time. A far-fetched solution would be to take *Primas* as Hugh (Primas) of Orleans, who 'despised the stones of his opponents' (instead of complaining): however, in *Dives eram et dilectus* (Wright, *Mapes*, pp. 64–9) Hugh does not mention stoning as one of his many grievances.

93. The MS. version may be translated 'Noah's flood subsided', but this is scarcely an *adynaton*; the theme of the stanza is that when Truth loves the ungrateful man several people noted for their virtue will prove to have been false. The emendation adopted implies that Noah was drowned along with the rest of guilty mankind.

94. St. Lawrence, martyred on a red-hot gridiron in A.D. 258; *reprobauerat* 'condemned, proved false'.

XLIX[1]

f. 76ᵇ   CONVENTUAL RATIONS

f. 76ᵇ   Sacrista p⟨re⟩cipit singulis diebus per annum duas iustas conventualis ceruisie et duas michas con-uentuales, et gastellos quando con⟨u⟩entus duplum recipit, et de coquina liberacionem duorum mona-chorum in omnibus.

Et hec omnia [per] Henricum Bleis, abbatem, pro operibus ecclesie assignata.

Henry de Blois, brother of Count Theobald and nephew of Henry I, was made Abbot in 1126; in 1129 he was promoted to the see of Winchester, but remained Abbot of Glastonbury until his death in 1171; for his rule at the abbey, his benefactions, and his work on the buildings, see John of Glastonbury, i. 165–70, where it is related (pp. 168–9) that:

quaedam ad recreacionem conventus liberaliter duxit adicienda. Dedit namque coquinae conventus augmentacionem decem solidorum sin-gulis septimanis per annum, molendinum de Strete, redditum viginti

---

[1] No. XLIX. *No title in MS.*   1 precipit: *MS.* percipit (per *abbreviated*). 3 conuentus: *minim too many between* o *and* e.

librarum piperis in urbe Londoniarum. Praeter haec, quia singulas principales festivitates Sanctae Mariae Dei genitricis multo devocius & solempnius solito, eius instinctu, fratres egerunt, atque post primum diem assumpcionis eiusdem virginis gloriosae, tres dies sequentes festive in capis, sicut in ebdomada Paschae & Pentecostes fit, cele-braverunt . . . liberaliter concessit conventui triginta salmones . . . etc.

These special allowances for feast-days are what is meant by *recipere duplum*. The *Benedictine Rule* stipulates the following allowances:

Ch. xxxix. 'De mensura cibi': Sufficere credimus ad refectionem cotidianam . . . cocta duo pulmentaria . . . et si fuerit unde poma aut nascentia leguminum, addatur et tertium. Panis libra una pro-pensa sufficiat in die, sive una sit refectio sive prandii et cenae . . . etc.
Ch. xl. 'De mensura potus': credimus heminam vini per singulos sufficere per diem. (No mention is made of beer.)

3–4 *et gastellos . . . recipit*: parenthetic, '. . . two ordinary convent loaves (and these are to be fine wastel-bread loaves when the abbey is giving a special entertainment).' For the phrase *duplum recipit*, see DC *receptum 1*, 'hospitality', *recipere*, 'receptum dare', *duplarium*, *duplices*, 'double feast(s), special feast-day(s)'.
4–5 *et de coquina . . . omnibus*: '. . . and as regards the kitchen, an allowance for two monks'; *in omnibus* may mean 'throughout the year, not just on special occasions'; for *liberatio* 'wages, allowance', see DC *liberare 2*.

L[1]

f. 77ᵃ   LETTER FROM COLOGNE FROM
NICHOLAS FROME

Carissimis confratribus suis Joh[anni ⟨Ledbury⟩] et Ricardo Busard' monachis Monasterii G[lastoniensis]

Nota quod omnes borones et nobiles Bohemie et marchionatus Morauie nuper post pascha circ[a] quartam ebdomadam, sencientes se subiectos per plebes et infimos populos heresi ista nephanda percussos, conuenerunt in vnum, et ducem Austrie

Albertum adierunt, cui quid⟨a⟩m ex eis fidelitate[m] iurarunt. 5
Quidam autem ex eis arbitrati sunt no[n] esse tutum talem
fidelitatem iurare pro tunc, qu[oniam] si iuramentum perciperetur a vulgo indocto, popul[i] ciuitatum et opidorum deficiliores
se redderent [a⟨d⟩] pacem minusque confiderent in ipsis baronibus, dum cum ipsis tractarent. Quare magis eis videbatur accom- 10
modum pro pace procuranda treugas vnire ad tempus, quod
eciam factum est.

Ceterum vero ipsi barones in vigilia Assencionis se invi-
[c⟨em⟩] congregantes in campo de mane iurarunt mutuo se non
deficere vsque ad mortem inclusiue, donec populum legi Dei, 15
ecclesie et hominum tam rebelle[m] predictis legibus subicerent ac hereticos Taborit[as], Orphanos et communicantes
sub vtraque interficerent, perimerent aut in exilium mitterent.

Vnde [⟨die⟩] Assencionis Domini hora quasi meri[di]ana
ingress[i] Pragam Veterem, habita prius bona fide cum c[i⟨ui- 20
bus⟩] eiusdem ciuitatis, secretissime tamen seruata ... sumpta
modica recreacione, statim ante horam secund[am] cum ciuibus
ingressi sunt isti domini barones ciuitat[em] Pragensem Nouam,
singulare habitaculum et speciale nidum hereticorum. Non
tamen ita caute ista fact[a] sunt quin ad aurem quorundam 25
istorum hereticorum perueniret horum propositum. Sed tam
subito irr[ue⟨runt⟩] domini barones et ciues predicti in illam
ciuitatem Nou[am], vt in foribus essent ciuitatis antequam
portas possent claudere. Quod videns Procopius Rasus, rector
in spiritualibus Taberitarum, statim fugit cum quatuordecim 30
equis.

Cristi militibus iam portas occupantibus nullus post eos
evadere poterat, quod videntes alii incole heretici ceperunt
f. 77b ascendere pretorium et domos forciores ciuitatis illius, pluribus
hinc inde in plateis alterius sanguibus balneatis, / aliis flumen 35
petentibus et in eodem submersis, paucissimis ad aliud litus
peruenientibus, sed hiis dominis baronibus a cede non cessantibus interfecti sunt senes cum iunioribus, mulieres cum pueris.
Inter quos interfectus est Lupus sacerdos eorum, potissimus

5 quidam: *MS.* quidem.

40 heresiarcha et impeditor per suas predicaciones omnis pacis et
concordie inter ecclesiam et illos. Videntes autem domini
barones quod tantus hereticorum populus domos fortissimas
occuparent et se laborabant defendere, posuerunt ignem ad
pretorium quod forcius erat, et quosdam combusserunt, quidam
45 se precipitauerunt; alii autem exeuntes se reddiderunt, ex quibus capitales statim mortui sunt gladio et aliis bellicis, et alii
carceribus mancipati sunt, et sic factum est de singulis qui
alias domos reciperent pro suis fo⟨r⟩taliciis. Modo quoque isto
liberata est ciuitas ista a malis habitatoribus, et nobiles domini
50 barones fideles milites ipsam inhabitant.

Hec vero audientes exercitus Boemiorum in numero decem
milia qui iam per vndecim menses opidum quoddam Boemie
dictum [⟨Pi⟩]lznam obciderunt, statim combustis tentoriis et
aliis defensionibus ligneis quibus se ab insultibus opidanorum
55 defenderant, recesserunt sine ordine vt homines confusi et
devicti. Et si affuissent de [bon]is viris CC equestres, plurimos
de exercitu vt creditur prostrassent, sed illi ciues obcessi duos
dumtaxat equos habuerunt infra ciuitatem. Ciues isti semper
manserunt fideles tanto tempore huius grauissime persecuci-
60 onis, et venientes ex hereticis ad eos vt suam heresim predi-
carent, quosdam igni tradiderunt, quosdam amputatis manibus
et erutis oculis ⟨ad⟩ suos patriarchos hereticos remiserunt,
racione cuius facti heretici acrius eos invaserunt, erantque eis
magis infesti, ignem minantes et mortem; sed Deus misertus est
65 populi sui et ipsos per vndecim menses adiuuit, vt in omnibus
insultibus cotidianis non sunt ex omnibus opidonis sex mortui,
pluribus ex hereticis prostratis, et tandem die sancta dominica /
f. 78ᵃ post Assencionem Domini placuit altissimo eos [eripe⟨re⟩] de
manibus inimicorum.

70   Acta sunt hec siue ista [in Bo⟨emia⟩] anno Domini millesimo
CCCCᵐᵒ xxxii⟨i⟩jᵒ circa festum Ascencionis Domini prout
superius annotatur. Et relata reu[e⟨ra⟩] coram toto consilio
Basilensi in congregacione gener[ali] die vicesima octaua Maii

48 fortaliciis: *MS.* foctaliciis.   62 ad: *MS.* et (*abbreviated*).
71 xxxiiij: *MS.* xxxiij.

per Reuerendum Magistrum dominum Johannem de Pallamore
auditorem curie apostoli[ce] et tunc legatum circa partes 75
Boemie ex parte con[s⟨ilii⟩] sacri predicti.

Et cognoscant vestre beneuole fraternitates quod [h⟨ec⟩] noua
habuimus in scriptis in Colonia in die Sanctor[um] Primi et
Feliciani, vbi per octo dies expectaui[mus] dominos sub-
sequentes. Ad quam ciuitatem accedentes xl miliaria propter 80
⟨g⟩uerras inter ducem Guldrie [et] ducem Montensem fuimus
in tanto periculo positi [⟨vt⟩] oporteret nos post Deum con-
fidere in archubus et sag[ittis], non obstantibus saluis conducti-
bus viuis et mortui[s]. Spem tamen posuimus, ponimus et
ponemus in suffrag[iis] Sanctorum ecclesie nostre et vestris 85
oracionibus specialem per q[ue] Deo duce salui et incolumes
preseruamur, quomodo reuertemur simpliciter ignorantes, si
non Deus [⟨quid⟩] solacii aliter disponat pro nobis. Nouem
[⟨Cardina⟩]les sunt in consilio: dominus Imperator est [⟨in
vrbe⟩] que vocatur Vlme super flumen Danubii; [⟨Summus⟩] 90
pontifex est in Roma. Et si nostri domini superv[enisse⟨nt⟩], nos
fuissemus in consilio vel prope, Deo duce, a[nte] datam pre-
sencium, vbi pluribus cognitis et auditis, posse[mus] dominos
nostros et vos de nouis contingentibus redder[e] cerciores.

Et quantum ad illa pertinet, retrahimu[s] calamum cum salute 95
intimis cordis nostri affectibus, desiderantes vt sancta religio,
quam in exitu nostr[o] pro tempore nostre absencie beneuole
promisistis, ad honorem Dei et profectum animarum vestrarum
continue convales[cat] et in gaudium amicorum et obprobrium
malignancium †c[um] tamen† mediis pacis et caritatis indies 100
augmentetur. Et de singulis pertinentibus ad gubernacionem
ecclesie exterius simpliciter confidimus in habentibus potes-
tatem. Et si fuerint inter vos nobis transmittenda, in posterum /
[⟨transm⟩ittantur] primo Londonias ad Alexandrum de Al- f.78b
bertinis, [quia] eius nuncii tempore ⟨g⟩uerre securius per- 105
transibunt. [Et] de singulis peragendis vestris occupacionibus,
presupposita sanitate, non intendimus vos per nostras litteras
fatigare.

81 guerras: *MS.* querras.　　100 cum tamen: *see Note.*　　105 eius:
MS. eius eorum. guerre: *MS.* querre.

Et si dominus meus singularissimus dominus Bathonensis vel
110 dominus de Hungerford ad vos declinauerint, ostendatis eis
vultum secundum vltimum potencie vestre. Et si maiores super-
venerint pro consilio habendo, mittatis ad dominum de Hungerford quamcito poteritis. Et salutetis merito salutandis, et
valeatis sicut nos vellemus nosipsos in corpore et anima vel
115 toto composito.

Scripte apud Coloniam in die Primi et Feliciani per
Nicholaum abbatem Glastoniensem.

Hec sunt nomina Cardinalium residencium in consilio:

Cardinalis Sancte ⟨Crucis⟩, primus presedens
120 Cardinalis Sancti Angeli, 2us presidens et legatus
Cardinalis Bononiensis
Cardinalis Placentinus
Cardinalis Rotomagensis
Cardinalis Arelatensis
125 Cardinalis Sancti Petri ad Vincula
Cardinalis Cipri
Cardinalis Firmanus.

Printed in Hearne's *Collections*, x. 139–41, 1 June 1729 (**H**); beginning and end transcribed by Richard James, Bodley MS. James 7,
pp. 84–8; photostat and discussion by A. N. E. D. Schofield,
'England and the Council of Basel' (London University Ph.D. thesis,
1956), Appendix 16 and pp. 269–70. The text is badly damaged, but
parts not now visible were read by Richard James and by Hearne.

Nicholas Frome (Abbot, 1420–56) writes from Cologne on 9 June
1434 (MS. 1433) to Richard Busard and John Ledbury, two Glastonbury monks who are otherwise unknown. Nicholas is on his way to
the Council of Basel, and first relates news (sent to him by letter)
narrated at the Seventeenth Session by John Palomar, Council dele-
gate in Bohemia: New Prague has fallen to the anti-Hussite alliance
of the nobles of Bohemia and Moravia, and the siege of Pilsen has
been raised. Nicholas says that he is now waiting at Cologne for the
remainder of the English delegation; his journey was dangerous
because of the war between the Dukes of Guelders and Berg; he
sends his good wishes to the abbey, and gives some instructions on

119 Crucis: *no gap in MS.*

how to write to him, and where to find advice in England on any problem concerning the abbey. After the colophon is a list of cardinals present at the Council: the list was probably attached to the letter.

The second English delegation to the Council of Basel (the first, formed in 1432, seems never to have left England) was chosen at Convocation, 7 Nov.–21 Dec. 1433; it left England on 18 June 1434 and arrived on 5 August: Frome must have left well ahead of the main party (he arrived in Cologne on 1 June). The Council had long been concerned with events in Bohemia, where, since the leadership of Žižka (d. 1424), the Hussite armies had had almost complete control. Their leader Procopius Magnus (Rasus) began to besiege Pilsen, the last major Catholic stronghold, in August 1433, but after a defeat by German troops at Wintersried and a revolt by his army he gave up the command, and returned to Prague. There the anti-Hussite nobles, under the leadership of Mainardus, had appointed Alscio of Risemberg as military leader; they began to stir up the conservative Old Town by inflammatory speeches. New Prague was fortified by Lupus of Ročyžana, a priest, but on 6 May the stronghold fell to the nobles and Lupus was killed. Procopius wrote to Procopius Parvus at Pilsen, advising him to abandon the siege. On 30 May 1434 the Hussite army was heavily defeated at Lipany, and Procopius Magnus and Parvus were killed (the English Hussite Peter Payne was captured: see *The Brut*, ed. F. W. D. Brie, EETS 136 (1908), pp. 502–3); the news of the battle of Lipany could not have been known to John of Palomar at the time of his announcement to the Council—he must have gone straight back from Pilsen to Basel.

WORKS REFERRED TO IN THE NOTES

Aeneas Sylvius (Pius II), 'De ortu et historia Bohemiorum', in *Aeneae Sylvii Piccolominei Senensis . . . opera* (Basel, 1571), pp. 81–143, partic. Ch. li 'De victoria Bohemorum fidelium et debellatione morteque Procopii ac aliorum haereticorum' (pp. 119 ff.).

Denis, E., *Huss et la guerre des Hussites* (Paris, 1878).

Eubel, C., *Hierarchia catholica medii aevi*, i. 1198–1431, ii. 1431–1503 (Münster, 1898–1901).

Haller, J., etc., *Concilium Basiliense: Studien und Dokumente*, 8 vols. (Basel, 1896–1936).

Hefele, C. J., and Leclerq, H., *Histoire des Conciles* (Paris, 1907–), vii (2).

Heymann, F. G., *John Žižka and the Hussite Revolution* (Princeton, 1955).

Mansi, J. D., etc., *Sacrorum Conciliorum Nova . . . Collectio* (Paris, 1759–), vol. xxx.

Palacký, F., *Urkundliche Beiträge zur Geschichte des Hussitenkrieges* (Prague, 1873).
Zellfelder, A., 'England u. das Basler Konzil', *Historische Studien*, ciii (1913), partic. pp. 239–311 (text of the *Codex Sprever*).

The name *Ledbury* was visible only to Richard James, not to Hearne.

1 ff. For an account of the activities of Mainardus in rousing the nobles against the Hussites, see Aeneas, p. 119. Easter 1434 was on 28 March.

1. *borones*: this spelling is recorded by *RWL*.

4–5. This projected alliance with Albert is not mentioned by Aeneas (who may have thought the implication of treachery unsympathetic to his ideas); however, Palacký (No. 905, p. 409) refers to, but does not print, a letter of 9 April 1434 on the subject of a possible alliance with Albert.

13. *in vigilia Assencionis*: 5 May 1434. Aeneas does not give the date of the sack of the New Town, but Palacký Nos. 910 and 911 (on this subject) are both dated in May.

17–18. *Taboritas et Orphanos et communicantes sub vtraque*: the Taborites (named after the Biblical Mount Tabor) were the first of the fanatical Hussite sects; after the death of John Žižka (the founder of the Hussite army) in 1424, his followers called themselves the 'Orphans'. The doctrine of taking communion 'in both kinds' (i.e. in wine as well as bread) was clearly enunciated in the second of the Four Articles of Prague (Denis, p. 494; Heymann, pp. 148–63): 'quod sacramentum divinissime eucharistie sub utraque specie, panis scilicet et vini, omnibus Christi fidelibus nullo peccato mortali indispositis libere ministretur.'

19. 6 May 1434.

21. None of the secrecy implied here is mentioned by Aeneas, who shows Alscio making a series of open challenges against the New Town, to which Lupus retaliated by blocking the ways out of the Old Town into the New. New Prague had been in Hussite hands since the beginnings of the movement: in 1419, for instance, it revolted under Žižka against an attempt by King Wenceslas to purge the city of all suspected of Hussite tendencies.

29. *Procopius Rasus*, also called *Magnus* to distinguish him from Procopius Parvus, was Žižka's successor as Taborite leader. Aeneas, probably misled by the names, implies that Procopius Magnus was present throughout at the siege of Pilsen, but the account of Czech chroniclers, that he left the siege in Autumn 1433 after a minor revolt against him by the army, is confirmed by the letter (Palacký, No. 908) from Magnus to Parvus after the fall of New Prague, advising the latter to raise the siege: clearly Magnus was not present at Pilsen—Nicholas's letter is additional confirmation.

34–5. '... many of them [lying] here and there in the streets, bathed in each other's blood.' *alterius* is better than **H** *alternis*; *sanguibus* (**H.** *sanguinibus*) is either an error or an analogical ablative plural. The syntax is loose: *pluribus* seems to be the first of a series of ablative absolute constructions ending at *cessantibus*.

39. *Lupus* of Ročyžana, priest and leader of the New Prague garrison. Aeneas does not record his death but says that he took flight when he saw the impending defeat.

51–2. *decem milia*: Procopius had between 12,000 and 18,000 men at the battle of Lipany (Heymann, p. 469).

53. *[Pi]lznam*: **H** . . . *bnam*, but Pilsen is clearly intended. Nicholas's 'opidum quoddam Boemie dictum . . .' shows that the siege was not as well known to the outside world as it was at the Council of Basel.

54. *defensionibus ligneis*: probably the famous Hussite war-wagons, developed into efficient fortress components by Žižka (description and picture in Heymann, p. 178).

58 ff. All chroniclers mention the difficulties of the besieged, but I have not seen elsewhere such circumstantial detail, nor the account of the treatment of the evangelizing Hussites.

67. *die sancta dominica*: 9 May 1434.

71. There can be no doubt that MS. *xxxiij* is a simple scribal error.

72 ff. The Seventeenth General Session had opened on 26 April in the presence of the Emperor Sigismond, who left on 19 May (Hefele-Leclerq, vii. 847, 867; cf. below). For an account of the jubilation at the reception of John of Palomar's news, see Haller, v (1904), 91; for letters from citizens of Pilsen and from Palomar to the Council, see Mansi, xxx. 828–9.

74. John of Palomar was appointed by Cardinal Julian Cesarini, head of the Council, his representative at Basel during the arrangements for the Council on 3 July 1431. After this Palomar was directly concerned with Bohemian affairs, and at least twice led a delegation to Prague (Hefele-Leclerq, vii. 789, 821, 858 ff.); he was sent to take help to Pilsen in Feb. 1434, and probably returned directly from there in May to give the news of the raising of the siege.

78–9. *die . . . Primi et Feliciani*: 9 June. Frome must have left England in April or early May, but the rest of the English delegation did not leave until 18 June; the whole party arrived together in Basel on 5 August (Zellfelder, p. 256).

80–2. 'We travelled forty miles to this town, and were placed in such extreme danger because of the wars between the Duke of Guelders and the Duke of Berg that . . .' In 1424 Arnold of Egmont became Duke of Guelders, and his title was recognized by the Emperor Sigismond, who in the next year revoked his decision and conferred the title on Adolf of Berg. In retaliation Arnold claimed the Duchy of Jülich, which had also been given to Adolf: a long war followed, and in 1433–4 Arnold attacked Jülich (with little success); it is to this war that Frome is referring; see *Algemene Geschiedenis der Nederlanden*, 12 vols. (Antwerp, 1949–58), iii, *De late Mitteleeuwen* (1951), 353.

82–4. 'We had to put our trust, after God, in bows and arrows, notwithstanding the safe conducts given to living and dead': *obstare* would normally mean 'hinder, prevent'; presumably *viuis* = 'noncombatants', *mortuis* = 'the enemy dead'.

87. The MS. capital *S* for *si* must be an error: '. . . having simply no idea how we are to return, unless God arranges some kind of comfort for us'.

89–90. One of the letters concerning the raising of the siege of Pilsen (Palacký, No. 910), dated 19 May 1434, was sent to Ulm, and is perhaps a copy of the letter sent to the Emperor, who had already left the Council.

91–4. *domini nostri* and *dominos nostros* refer to two different sets of people: 'if our colleague delegates had arrived, we would have been at the Council, by God's guidance, before the date of the present letter or nearly so, and would have been more able, having heard and learnt more information, to inform you and our superiors [? the Archbishop Chichele] about the news.' Frome's impatience was perhaps justified, considering that the English delegation had been formed 7 Nov.–21 Dec. 1433.

100. *c[um]* (so **H**) is at the end of the line; at the beginning of the next line the MS. has *tū* (*tum*) or *tñ* (*tamen*). It is tempting to assume that **H**'s *cum* was an error, and to reconstruct *t[an]tum*. The sense of the line is: '. . . and that to the joy of our friends and the shame of our detractors religion may increase by means [*mediis*] of love and peace continually.' For *cum tamen mediis* the printed text of Hearne's *Collections* reads *cum remediis*: this is Salter's emendation (or misreading) and not Hearne's.

104–5. *Alexandrum de Albertinis*: I have been unable to identify him.

107. *presupposita sanitate*: 'assuming that you are in good health.'

109–10. *Dominus Bathonensis* and *d. de Hungerford* were both highranking treasury ministers under Henry VI; the former was John Stafford (d. 1452), Bishop of Bath and Wells, 1425–43, Archbishop of Canterbury, 1443–52. Sir Walter (Lord) Hungerford was English envoy to the Council of Constance, 1414, successor to Stafford in the treasury until 1432, became Baron Hungerford, 1426, d. 1449 (*DNB*).

110–11. The phrase *vultum ostendere* may be modelled on the ME *make chere*, 'greet well, favourably' (see *MED*), but *secundum*, adj., may have been omitted by haplography.

118 ff. The accuracy of this list for the time of the arrival of the English delegation is confirmed by the *Codex Sprever* (Zellfelder, op. cit.), which gives an account of the cardinals whom the English party visited. Their names are to be found in Eubel:

119. *Sancte Crucis*: Nicholas de Albergatis, nominated joint-president of the Council by Eugenius IV (who recognized the Council in Dec. 1433).

120. *Sancti Angeli*: Julian Cesarini, the first president of the Council, nominated by Martin V in Jan. 1431, and its leader during the struggles with Eugenius IV.

121. *Bononiensis* (Bologna): Antonius Corrarius.

122. *Placentinus* (Piacenza): Branda de Castiglione, another early member.

123. *Rotomagensis* (Rouen): Johannes de Ruppescissa.

124. *Arelatensis* (Arles): Ludovicus Alamandi.

125. *Sancti Petri (ad Vincula)*: Johannes Cervantes.

126. *Cipri*: Hugo de Lusignano, son (later brother) of the King of Cyprus.

127. *Firmanus* (Fermo): Dominicus de Capranica.

All the nine cardinals were appointed in the creations of Martin V in 1419 and 1426, except Corrarius (Gregory XII, 1408) and Castiglione (John XXIII, 1411).

ADDENDUM[1]

SINCE the printing of the first proofs, the following information has come to my attention. The manuscript from which Wright made his transcript (**W**) has been rediscovered: it is Wellcome Historical Medical Library MS. 406 (the 'Loscombe MS.'). See Arne Zettersten, *The Virtues of Herbs in the Loscombe Manuscript: a contribution to Anglo-Irish language and literature* (Lund: Acta Universitatis Lundensis, Sectio I, Theologica, Juridica, Humaniora, 5, 1967). The Loscombe MS. is, on linguistic evidence, Anglo-Irish. The poem, which is its fourth item, consists of 272 lines, of which Wright transcribed 205–72. Roughly speaking, the first part of the Loscombe text of the poem (1–120) corresponds to the opening of the poem 'The Virtues of Herbs' (*Index Suppl.* 3754); its second part, 123–241 corresponds to 'T' 83–196; it concludes with *1–*31 as printed here on pp. 110–11. Thus T 1–82 is not found elsewhere, and at no point does the text of T correspond to any version of 'The Virtues of Herbs' other than its unique form in the Loscombe MS. The exact history of the poem still remains unclear. I am inclined to regard the Loscombe version as a conflation of two originally distinct poems.

[1] See above, p. 109.

APPENDIX II

LATER ADDITIONS TO THE MS.[1]

In this Appendix are included all later entries made in the MS. by hands **X**, **A**, and **B**, excluding titles, page-headings, marginal notes, etc. (see above, pp. 5–6). Nos. *1–*4 were made on ff. 1ª, 88ᵇ, and 89ᵇ by hand **X**: these entries were probably made in the fifteenth century (for the date 1475, see below, pp. 141–2). Nos. *5–*19 were made by hand **A**; from changes in nib, ink, etc., the probable order of the entries can be determined: *11, *12, *13, *15, *17, *18, *16, *6, *8, *5, *7, *9, *19, *10, and *14 (Nos. *10 and *14 may have preceded *8, etc.). It is evident from his corrections to the entries by **T** that the writer of **A** was very learned: the damaged note *11 may give the name of **A** as Sowdene or John Pydsloy. The **A** entries were made in the early years of Elizabeth's reign, the latest (*14) not before 4 June 1561. The five proverbs by hand **B** are dated later than **A** on palaeographical grounds only: it is possible that the same person made the **A** and **B** entries, but it should be noted that an emendation begun by **A** on f. 4ᵇ has been completed by **B**.[2] Entries by both **A** and **B** were transcribed by Twyne in or after 1634.

Hand X

f. 1ª   *1

(*a*) Four Latin lines of proverbial weather-lore, expressing the theme 'red sky at night, . . .', etc. Cf. Walther 13583, *Sprichw.* 20577; Harley 3362 (xvi c.), f. 31ᵇ; *Hortulus anime* (Antwerp, 1596, Bodley Douce A. 59), f. 20ª; Werner *Beiträge*, p. 176.

(*b*) A short Latin prose passage recounting the journey of the soul after death: it is given a seven-day tour of creation (heaven, hell, etc.), and is addressed by the sins it committed, before its *judicium*

---

[1] The later entries are printed in full, with annotation, thesis, ii. 442–60.
[2] II. 216. The emendation coincides with the reading of MS. Cotton Vespasian E. xii. In some of these annotations and corrections the handwriting is similar to that of Twyne himself (see above, p. 7), and it is possible that some of them (including this emendation) are not by **A** but by Twyne. The additions by **A** cannot, of course, be by Twyne, who himself transcribed No. *13.

privatum (as distinct from the Last Judgement); I have seen no notice of the passage elsewhere, but it is also in Digby 88, f. 1ᵇ (with only slight differences from **X**). The passage opens with *Agustinus dicit*, but I have been unable to trace it in Augustine's works: Augustine makes no mention of this 'tour' when he is speaking of the *judicium privatum* (*In Joannis evangelium*, *PL* xxxv. 1751; *De rectitudine catholicae conversationis*, *PL* xl. 1183–4).

f. 1ᵃ   *2

The changes of the moon, probably from a calendar.

f. 88ᵇ   *3

Nota de Epistola ad papam missa dum erat in missa: In Anglissis' verbis in modo hoc: In Clent Cowbachi Kennelme Kyngysbyrth lyth vndyre thoryne beheddyde.

In Clent vacce valle Kennelmus Regius natus jacet sub spina decapitatus. Epistola de Sancto Kynelmo Regi.

This note is known to have circulated separately in MSS., e.g. Pembroke College, Cambridge, MS. 82: see N. R. Ker, *Catalogue of MSS. containing Anglo-Saxon* (1957), p. 124. It is part of the very popular legend of St. Kenelm: the letter to the Pope revealed the location of the murdered body of the saint. The English lines, where they are given in full, clearly show an OE alliterative pattern. For a full account, see thesis, ii. 454–5, and *Early Middle English Verse and Prose*, ed. J. A. W. Bennett and G. V. Smithers, with a Glossary by Norman Davis (1966), pp. 96–107, 312–16: this prints the *SEL* version of the story (i. 279–91), with full notes and bibliography. There were three Latin translations of the verses: the one found here (also in *NLA* ii. 110–13), and two (one by John de Cella, Abbot of St. Alban's) in Matthew Paris's *Chronica Majora*, ed. H. R. Luard, 7 vols., RS lvii (1872–83), i. 373, and the *Flores Historiarum*, ed. H. R. Luard, 3 vols., RS xcv (1890), i. 411–12.

f. 89ᵇ   *4

Four very damaged items: the first two are Latin proverbs, the second (improbably attributed to Augustine) against back-biting; the third is an English prayer by the Holy Name (*Index* and *Suppl.* 1703: eighteen MSS. are recorded, including this one); the fourth is an English remark on the preceding prayer, granting indulgence to anyone who says it: the last line reads 'Mˡ C.C.C.C. lxxv yerys', which may refer to the length of the indulgence or to the date on which the entry was made—1475 would be a very suitable date for the entries by hand **X**.

Hand **A**

f 76ᵇ   *5

The lover true
In colour blew
  Hymmeselfe he dothe adorne;
The virgyne brighte
All whyte in sighte;
  The sadde in black dothe morne;
The lustye greane
Right well besene
  Betokenethe the flowers of yowthe;
The manne forsaken
In tawney is shapen,
  As a manne full of ruthe;
The ioyfull yellowe
The redde dothe folowe,
  For anger as hote as fyre;
The russett hue
Hopythe to ensue
  The fruytz of hys desyre.
            Finis quod R. Jax

Index Suppl. 3416.5: not found elsewhere. What appears to be an *x* (in accordance with the normal letter-form of **A**) could also be an abbreviation; the name might also be *Jacques*. The colour symbolism appears to be popular rather than learned; for the latter, cf. Glynne Wickham, *Early English Stages*, 2 vols. (1959), i. 45–9.

f. 7ᵇ   *6

The tenthe day of October Aº 2º Eliz. Frenche Crownes and pystyletz were cryed lesse by a grote, so yᵗ the French Crowne was butt viˢ, the the pystylett vˢ xᵈ.

Transcribed by Hearne, *Collections*, x. 141. For measures taken against the drain of English currency abroad, see E. Lipson, *Economic History of England*, vol. iii, *The Age of Mercantilism*, 3rd edn. (1943), pp. 80–4, and R. H. Tawney and E. Power, *Tudor Economic Documents*, 3 vols. (1924), ii. 182–4, iii. 346–59.

f. 82ᵃ *7

A° i Eliz. xxiij° Januarij A° domini 1558
We berdlesse menne that are your sheape
And shorne att your request,
Revylen the and spyten the
And cownt the for a beast.

The date (= 1559) cannot be that on which the entry was made in the MS., if the above assumptions about the order of entries are correct.

f. 85ᵇ *8

Questio
When shall your cruell stormez be past?
Shall nott my truthe your rigor slake?
I wyll nomore whyle lyfe dothe last
Medell with love, butt ytt forsake,
With-owt yow answere and reherse
The first word of euery verse.

Respons
When stormez be past, the calme is next;
Tyme temperyth all things in euery place.
Dothe nott the wysemann teache hys text
'Serue truly—therof comythe grace'?
Yow are no foole: your wylye brayne
Shall serue to fynde my answere playne.

Index Suppl. 4014.5 records this MS. only, but these acrostic poems are also in Harley 78, f. 30ᵃ and Rawlinson poet. 108, f. 11ᵇ, with minor variations only.

f. 86ᵃ *9

Wylt thow and I by one assent—
Thow thieselfe shall chuse or no—
Thatt thow and I be bothe content?
I wyll the same, yf thow wylt so.
Shall hytt be so, goodde? lett me know.
Jape on who lyst, for earnyst I meane:
The yea geavythe lyfe, the nay kyllethe playne.

f. 86ᵃ *10

Seldome seene ys swetyst,
    and pretye thingis be strange;
Dyuers dyshes are metyst
    for them thatt loven change.

f. 86ᵇ   *11

The top left-hand (outer) corner of the leaf is missing. The ends of the
first two lines read: . . . *Sowdene hunc librum* and . . . [*m*]*agistri Jo.*
Pydsloy possidet. As these lines are probably the first entry by **A**
they may well indicate the ownership of the MS., but it is difficult
to interpret them exactly. They are followed by a short Latin prose
note, also badly damaged and impossible to interpret.

f. 86ᵇ   *12

Two lists of the Kings of England, the first a short mnemonic, the
second a full-length list; the second ends with *Elizabethe*, the first
Henque modernus, i.e. 'and the late Henry [the Eighth]': the sense
'the late' is given by *RWL*. Both lists were corrected and expanded
by **A** after he made list *18. Both begin with William the Conqueror.

f. 87ᵃ   *13

  Epita[phium in Gressamum]
  Scribere cur cess[am miseri de funere Gressham ?]
  Qui longe in terra viu[ebat quasi viuerra]

   . . . .

  Et tu, O London, ferme que fueras v[ndon],
  Jubilate Deum, quia demon possidet [eum!]

  Responsio Ry. Sherrij ad ep . . .
  illi adscriptum et aduersus . . .
  Qui rythmos scripsit miseros de fune[re . . .]
  Scurra fuit petulans, vappa malig[n . . .]

   . . . . .

  Inveheris quod agros iuste sine fraude paravit,
  Prediaque in variis possidet ille locis.

Ed. A. G. Rigg, *Guildhall Miscellany*, vol. ii, No. 9 (August, 1967),
389–91; thesis, ii. 449–50, 457–9; otherwise unnoticed since Twyne,
whose transcript (see above p. 7) enables us to restore most of the
lines. The first (anonymous) poem is in dog-Latin Leonine hexameters (24 lines), and is a vicious and scurrilous attack on the late
Sir Richard Gresham (d. 1549), father of the financier: his assistance
(partly as Lord Mayor) in the seizure of Catholic hospitals in the City
and in the persecution of Protestants must have earned him widespread hatred. See J. W. Burgon, *Life and Times of Sir Thomas*
Gresham, 2 vols. (1839), i. 21–43. The reply (which appears to be
incomplete) is by the writer on poetic theory, Richard Sherry
(d. 1555: see *DNB* for his biography); there are 16 lines.

f. 87ᵃ   *14

The iiij^th of June beinge Corpus eve, the thyrde yeare of quene
. . . A° domini 1561, Powles was burn[t] with lyghtenynge which
began at . . . a clock in the after none att the toppe of the Stepell
and so burnyd downard all thatt night vntyll . . . hole churche
was bur . . .

On the burning of St. Paul's in 1561, see: 'Vera Historia Incendii
Templi Sancti Pauli London' (from Bishop Grindal's Register),
'The Trve Report of the Burnynge of the Steple and Churche of
Poules in London', and a ballad, 'The Burning of Paules', all
printed by W. S. Simpson, *Documents Illustrating the History of St.
Paul's Cathedral*, CS, N.S. xxvi (1880), and also G. H. Cook, *Old
St. Paul's Cathedral* (1955), pp. 77–8.

f. 87ᵇ   *15–*16

Three English medical recipes, the first (*15) badly damaged and
missing its title, the next two (*16) respectively 'for the gowte' and
'for the gravell and stone'. *16(b), the shortest, is almost all visible.

f. 88ᵃ   *17

Note on the regnal dates of Mary Tudor and the accession and
coronation of Queen Elizabeth.

f. 89ᵃ   *18

Another list of kings from William the Conqueror to Elizabeth, with
their claims to the throne.

f. 89ᵇ   *19

Damaged and indecipherable note, perhaps a verse couplet: most of
the page is lost.

Hand B

                                *20

f. 9ᵃ   (i) Qui capit vxorem litem capit atque dolorem
f. 28ᵇ   (ii) fallere flere nere tria sunt hec in muliere
f. 63ᵇ   (iii) Seruicium pueri mulieris et monachorum
               Est et semper erit lytell thancke in fine laborum

          (iv)   Conuersio Sancti Pauli
               Clara dies Pauli bona tempora denotat anni
               Si fuerint venti designat prelia genti
               Si nix vel pluuia designat tempora chara
               Si fuerint næbulæ pereunt animalia queque.

(v)   Purificacio beate Marie
Clara dies si sit Maria purificante
Glacies maior erit tunc postea quam fuit ante.

These proverbs are entered in appropriate places among the entries
by **T**: (i) is added after the colophon to No. III, 'De Poena Coniugii';
(ii) is written above the penultimate stanza of No. 12 (which expands
this proverb); (iii), (iv), and (v) are interspersed among the proverbs
by **T** on f. 63ᵇ (No. XLIII).

(i) Walther *Sprichw.* 23903–6. Werner *Sprichw.*[2] Q 69, p. 98.

(ii) Walther *Sprichw.* 8751; see Skeat, *EEP*, No. 267, Chaucer
CT WBP III (D), 401–2 (and Robinson's note), *Crooked Rib*, pp. 3–4.

(iii) Walther *Sprichw.* 28175, recording Harley 3362, f. 2ᵃ (slightly
different); also in T.C.C. O.2.40, f. 120ᵇ. Cf. **T**'s No. XLIII(a), above
p. 88, and Erasmus, *De Recta Pronuntiatione* (1528: Bodley shelf-
mark Byw. M 6. 24), pp. 18–19.

(iv) Walther 2825, *Sprichw.* 2788, Werner *Sprichw.*[2] C 46 (p. 28),
Robbins *SL*, p. 247; to Walther's references add Harley 3362, f. 31ᵇ,
and T.C.C. O.2.53, f. 74ᵃ.

(v) Not in Walther or *Sprichw.*; also found in Harley 3362, f. 31ᵇ.

FIRST LINE INDEX OF VERSE

BIBLIOGRAPHICAL INDEX

AH	*Analecta Hymnica*, ed. G. M. Dreves and C. Blume, 55 vols. (Leipzig, 1886–1922).
Anglia	*Anglia: Zeitschrift für englische Philologie.*
Anzeiger	*Anzeiger für Kunde der deutschen Vorzeit.*
Archiv	*Archiv für das Studium der neueren Sprachen.*
Babees Book	*The Babees Book, etc.*, ed. F. J. Furnivall, EETS, 32 (1868).
Bannatyne MS.	*The Bannatyne MS.*, ed. W. T. Ritchie, 4 vols., STS, N.S. xxii, xxiii, xxvi, 3rd ser. v (1928–33).
Beiträge	see Werner.
Benedictine Rule	*Sancti Benedicti Regula Monasteriorum*, ed. D. C. Butler, 2nd edn. (Freiburg, 1927).
Brown	see *EL XIII, RL XIV, RL XV, Register.*
BRUO	Emden, A. B., *Biographical Register of the University of Oxford to 1500*, 3 vols. (1957–9).
Carm. Bur.	*Carmina Burana*, ed. A. Hilka and O. Schumann, vols. i, 1–2, ii, 1 (Heidelberg, 1930–41).
Carm. prov.	*Carminum proverbialium . . . loci communes* (1588: Douce P. 622).
Catalogue	see James.
Chaucer	*Works of Geoffrey Chaucer*, ed. F. N. Robinson, 2nd edn. (Boston, Mass., 1957): abbreviations on p. 647 are followed here. Reference is occasionally made to *The Oxford Chaucer*, ed. W. W. Skeat, 7 vols. (1894–7).
Chevalier	Chevalier, U., *Repertorium Hymnologicum*, 6 vols. (Louvain, 1892–1921).
CLP	Raby, F. J. E., *History of Christian-Latin Poetry*, 2nd edn. (1953).
CMEL	*Cambridge Middle English Lyrics*, ed. H. A. Person (Seattle, 1953).
Collections	see Hearne.
Crooked Rib	Utley, F. L., *The Crooked Rib: an analytical index* (Columbus, 1944).
CS	Camden Society.
DC	Du Cange, *Glossarium mediae et infimae latinitatis*, ed. L. Favre (Paris, 1883–7).
DNB	*Dictionary of National Biography.*

Wright *Latin Stories*   *Selection of Latin Stories*, ed. T. Wright, Percy
                         Soc. viii (1842).
Wright *Mapes*   *Latin Poems commonly attributed to Walter
                         Mapes*, ed. T. Wright, CS xvi (1841).
Wright *Pol. Poems*   *Political Poems and Songs*, ed. T. Wright, 2
                         vols., RS xiv (1859).
Wright *Pol. Songs*   *Political Songs of England . . . John to . . .
                         Edward II*, ed. T. Wright, CS vi (1839).

INDEX OF MANUSCRIPTS

GENERAL INDEX

PRINTED IN GREAT BRITAIN
AT THE UNIVERSITY PRESS, OXFORD
BY VIVIAN RIDLER
PRINTER TO THE UNIVERSITY